THE BOOK OF BOTTOMS

There is, it would appear, something of a conspiracy against the majestic bottom and its proper appreciation. *The New York Times* lately banned a good-humoured advertisement for 'Charlie' perfume which depicted a girl about to plant a playful pat on a man's rump; in Britain the Advertising Standards Authority likewise condemned a similar cinema ad for Southern Comfort.

So it is that the humble bottom-fancier (whether male or female) has in recent years risked being misclassified as some kind of degenerate weirdo. Such a conclusion would be altogether iniquitous. The honest appreciation of bottoms is an inalienable human pleasure, as old as the oldest of our human instincts. It is high time to end all this bigotry about our rear ends, and to restore 'Rumpus Rex' to its pre-eminent status as an object *par excellence* of pulchritude, enchantment and exhilaration. Despair no more, bottom-fanciers. The Book of Bottoms will strike a resounding blow for all of you, everywhere!

ABOUT THE AUTHOR

Joe Da Vinci was born in Sellafield, Cumbria, the son of Italian-South African immigrants who ran the staff canteen for scientists working on Britain's 'Atoms for Peace' programme to develop nuclear weapons. After a critical but highly active childhood he joined the family business and eventually became embroiled in the notorious 'Plutonium for Pasta' scandal which caused him to fall-out with his family and led to his discharge into the nearby environment.

It was on a low-level mission to South Africa, where he was exploring the market for self-cooking pasta, pizza and lamb, that he first fell under the hypnotic spell of Geronimus L. Grimes, world-famous clunologist. Joe immediately dumped his nuclear career and in a short time became one of the world's hindmost authorities on rear ends. He is regularly invited to give demonstration lectures in many countries, and has a consultancy business fronted by a sandwich bar which is discreetly patronised by the South African Bureau of State Security and most of the nuclear industry.

The Book of Bottoms

Joe Da Vinci

With cartoons by
Tim Baker

NEW ENGLISH LIBRARY
HODDER AND STOUGHTON

Copyright © 1989 Q.C.C. Co. Ltd
Illustration copyright
© Tim Baker 1989

First published in Great Britain in 1989 by New English Library paperbacks

A New English Library paperback original

This book is sold subject to the condition that it shall not, by way of trade or otherwise, be lent, re-sold, hired out or otherwise circulated without the publisher's prior consent in any form of binding or cover other than that in which it is published and without a similar condition including this condition being imposed on the subsequent purchaser.

No part of this publication may be reproduced or transmitted in any form or by any means, electronically or mechanically, including photocopying, recording or any information storage or retrieval system, without either the prior permission in writing from the publisher or a licence, permitting restricted copying. In the United Kingdom such licences are issued by the Copyright Licensing Agency, 33-4 Alfred Place, London WC1E 7DP.

British Library C.I.P.

Da Vinci, Joe
  The book of bottoms.
  I. Title
  828'.91409

ISBN 0-450-50810-2

Printed and bound in Great Britain for Hodder and Stoughton paperbacks, a division of Hodder and Stoughton Ltd., Mill Road, Dunton Green, Sevenoaks, Kent TN13 2YA (Editorial Office: 47 Bedford Square, London WC1B 3DP) by Cox & Wyman. Typeset by Avocet Robinson, Buckingham.

ACKNOWLEDGEMENTS

Grateful thanks are due to the caucus of clunologists who have selflessly offered the (sometimes over-ripe) fruits of a lifetime's dedicated perusal of posteriors, chief among whom are Barry, Bernard, Colin, Tim and – of course – the paragon of professional pygal pervestigators, Professor G. L. Grimes.

Joe Da Vinci.
London 1989

CONTENTS

List of Photographs	ix
Introduction	xi
1: The Joy of Bottoms	1
2: Bottom Spotting for Beginners	31
3: Cherish That Bottom!	83
4: The Hall of Fame	101
5: The Hall of Shame	103
6: The Clunology Quiz	105
7: A Bun is for Fun!	115
Answers to the Clunology Quiz	125
Photograph Credits	131

PHOTOGRAPHS

1. Brigitte Nielson in line-up on beach
2. Lulu in blue jumpsuit
3. Madonna in Japan
4. Diana Ross in concert
5. Marilyn Monroe and Jane Russell in costume in *Gentlemen Prefer Blondes*
6. Samantha Fox sunbathing
7. John Curry performing a jump-kick on ice
8. Ed Moses at start of hurdles race
9. Competitor in Mr. Universe contest
10. The Prince of Wales at a polo match
11. Rear view of heavily-tattooed man
12. Ronald Reagan boarding aeroplane at Seattle
13. Mohammed Ali in training
14. Elton John
15. Bette Midler in a wheelchair in mermaid costume
16. Joan Collins and fan in 'Acid' t-shirt
17. Jackie Onassis doing yoga
18. Yoko Ono and Anthony Cox with 'model'
19. The Duchess of York on ski slope
20. Girl with tattoos of the Duke and Duchess of York outside Buckingham Palace

INTRODUCTION

Rumpus Rex

A lofty buttock bared with azure veins,
Whose comely swelling, when my hand distrains,
It makes the fruits of love eftsoon be ripe;
And pleasure plucked too timely from the stem
To die ere it has seen Jerusalem.
                      Thomas Nashe, 1567–1601,
                      The Choice of Valentines

No, they don't write poems like that any more. In fact, in today's world the 'lofty buttock bared with azure veins' which so overstimulated the untimely Thomas Nashe is mightily under-celebrated. There is, it would appear, something of a conspiracy against the majestic bottom and its proper appreciation. A few recent examples will prove the case: the *New York Times* lately banned a good-humoured advertisement for 'Charlie' perfume which depicted a girl about to plant a playful pat on a man's rump; in Britain the Advertising Standards Authority likewise condemned a similar cinema ad for Southern Comfort. And a British doctor recently found himself suspended from practising medicine for eight long months while the General Medical Council investigated an unorthodox technique – namely, spanking – which he found to be highly effective in relieving sexual guilt, reducing general tension and as a cure for persistent smokers. In his defence, the peppy physician stated that his treatment was based entirely on St Paul's epistle to the Hebrews, which taught that chastisement was unpleasant but brought peace. Happily, he was eventually reinstated. 'I am delighted,' said the good doctor on learning of his acquittal, 'and I'm just looking forward to getting back to work.' You betcha.

So it is that the humble bottom-fancier (whether male or female) has in recent years risked being misclassified as some kind of degenerate weirdo. Such a conclusion would be altogether iniquitous. The honest appreciation of bottoms is an inalienable human pleasure, as old as the oldest of our human instincts. It is high time to end all this bigotry about our rear ends, and to restore 'Rumpus Rex' to its preeminent status as an object *par excellence* of pulchritude, enchantment and exhilaration. Despair no more, bottom-fanciers. *The Book of Bottoms* will strike a resounding blow for all of you, everywhere!

1

THE JOY OF BOTTOMS

Buttocks, big sisters of the breasts, more natural
And open, parted in a candid smile,
So simple they don't care to bully or beguile,
All their dictatorship simply being beautiful.
Paul Verlaine 1844—96

Bum-Words

(The author is indebted to Professor G. L. Grimes for granting permission to reprint the following essay, which serves as an excellent introduction to cluneal vocabulary, and is taken from Bowels and Vowels: A Modern Perspective, *Sjambok Press, 1984)*

The human race has always enjoyed a paradoxical love-hate relationship with its rear end, which no doubt reflects the two very different uses to which it is put — public titillation and private elimination. Yet, despite near-heroic efforts to banish bottom-words from polite society, they stubbornly refuse to roll over and die. This raises two very peculiar points about the terminology of the rear end — firstly, every 'bum-word' will sooner or later become so defiled and vulgarised that morally upright people will seek to ostracise it from their vocabulary; and secondly, no matter how vigorous or thorough the process of cleansing, new bottom-words invariably spring up thicker and faster than ever before. No sooner has one word been successfully deported than a whole host of newcomers seem to invade the language. Take the word 'arse', for instance. It is a venerable old word, and the oldest 'bum-word' which is still in common use. 'Arse' can be traced at least as far back as 1000 A.D., and is clearly related to the Anglo-Saxon word *ears*, the Icelandic and Swedish *ars*, the Danish *arts* and the German *arsch*. In the fourteenth century, Chaucer used the word without the slightest embarrassment – notably in an hilarious incident in *The Miller's Tale*. Absolon, an amorous suitor, thinking that he is about to win a kiss from the object of his passion, is tricked on a dark night into kissing the bottom she extends from her bedroom window. 'With his mouth he kissed her naked arse full savoury,' Chaucer relates, but Absolon knows something is wrong, because 'For well he knew a woman hath no beard – he felt a thing all rough and long-haired.' Later, the woman's real lover (called Nicholas) tries to repeat the trick, with very different results. Absolon is not going to be fooled a second time, and is waiting with a red-hot poker. When Nicholas sticks his bottom out of the window, Absolon 'was ready with his iron hot, and Nicholas amid the arse he smote'.

The phrase 'kiss my arse' has traditionally been used to repel the devil. It seems that in many folklore cultures, the devil has no bottom at all but, where his bottom should be, he instead sports another face. Now, when the devil goes about his wicked work of tempting all and sundry it is thought that he can be driven away by saying the simple phrase 'kiss my arse'. This is supposed to create a state of profound jealousy in the devil, who naturally enough, suffering from a lack of bottom, cannot return the challenge and therefore scuttles embarrassedly away without accomplishing his evil intention. The phrase was eventually considered unnecessary and it was deemed sufficient to show the devil your arse if you wished to drive him away. This was a favourite method of Martin Luther, who was, it seems, often visited with temptations. Similarly, statues were once positioned, and still may be seen, on the outsides of buildings in poses which had them displaying their buttocks outward to all who passed – thus warding off the devil. Both phrase and action have retained their popularity (and effectiveness?) for centuries, although the phrase has become 'kiss my ass' and the action has amended so that complete display is not essential, gestures and physical insinuations sufficing instead.

Other bygone usages of the word 'arse' also indicate that the word was once as socially acceptable as any other. Our modern proverb 'the pot calling the kettle black' originally started life as 'the pot calling the kettle black arse', but was presumably attenuated by some pre-Victorian proverb-purifier. Similarly, the saying 'You'd lose your head if it were loose' also started out as the altogether earthier 'You'd lose your arse if it were loose' and, again, received attention from the censor somewhere in the past two or three centuries. Old words such as 'arse-upwards' (meaning good luck), 'arse-board' (tail board of a cart) and 'arsy-versy' (now watered-down to become 'topsy-turvy') also bear witness to the democratic tradition of arse-words in the English vocabulary. The 'arse of a tree' was the expression used to describe the rough root-end after the roots had been chopped off. A house built in an isolated spot was considered by Suffolk people to be at the 'arse end of the world'. Arse could even be used as a verb meaning to move backwards, as in 'arse back your horse'. Country folk who wished to protect their houses against fire could write a spell on the side of their house called an 'arse-verse'. And when bakers used a long pole to spread hot embers over all parts of their oven, they called it an 'arsling-pole' (arsling meaning to move backwards).

By the time of Shakespeare, 'arse' was still in common parlance, although getting decidedly smuttier. In *A Midsummer Night's Dream*, Shakespeare obviously intends a visual pun on the word 'bottom' by giving the character with that name the head of an ass (which sounds like arse). However, Shakespeare uses the word 'bum', which probably originates from the noise an expulsion of wind generates, in preference to 'arse', so we may assume that by then 'arse' was definitely on its way out. 'Anus', first used in the middle of the seventeenth century, soon became the accepted term of reference for the rear end, and having a Latin pedigree, somehow acquired an aloof and semi-technical flavour which it still possesses to this day. Like 'arse' before it, 'bum' was at first a socially acceptable word – the *Dictionary of the Vulgar Tongue*, published in 1811, recounts the story of an upright young lady who refused to use the description 'jack ass' on account of its indecency, but who was more than happy to substitute 'johnny bum' for it!

'Bum' gave rise to a great many variants and descendants before it, too, fell from grace. There were 'bum bags' for trousers, 'bum bailiff' for an officer of the law, 'bum bass' for a cello, 'bum brusher' for a schoolmaster well versed in the science of corporal punishment, 'bum shop' for brothel, 'bum perisher' for a short-tailed coat, 'bum roll' for a woman's bustle, and 'bum sucker' for a sycophant (similar to the contemporary 'arse-licker').

Today, neither 'arse' nor 'bum' are wholly legitimate words. They have been largely superseded by slicker, fresher words (such as tush, buns, butt, hindquarters, fanny, bucket and stump) which still have the superficial gloss of newness about them, and not so much of the hoary old associations which straight-laced folk seem to find so abhorrent. Words such as 'butt' or 'fanny' (both current Americanisms for bottom) are certainly more socially acceptable than 'arse', which has a rank, almost indecent lewdity about it in comparison. Perhaps our society feels the need to change its verbal underpants from time to time, in an attempt to escape from the more earthy, malodorous aspects of our human natures. Nevertheless, a culture isn't changed as easily as all that. Try as we may to distance ourselves from the flesh-and-blood words of our language, they steadfastly refuse to be entirely exorcised. In fact, they're forever lurking under the surface, ready to materialise with a smirk and a leer at any moment.

For example, take the expression 'country bumpkin', still frequently used to describe someone of unsophisticated demeanour. When the morally chaste and virtuous use this rather twee little expression, do they realise, one wonders, the full meaning of the phrase? Look no further than the first three letters of the second word. 'And so I take my leave,' wrote a wit in the seventeenth century. 'Prithee, sweet thumkin – hold up thy coats, that I may kiss thy bumpkin.'

The Original Country Bumpkin

And when was the last time you described a bad experience as a 'bummer'? It's not a hang-over from the days of flower-power. The word actually comes, rather indirectly, from 'bum', meaning tail-end, and was first applied to the stragglers and hangers-on who attached themselves to General Sherman's march from Atlanta to the sea during the American civil war. Thus the American word 'bum' means a sponger or a tramp, and, through a circuitous route, ultimately has its roots in the English word 'bum,' meaning rear-end.

We all suffer from 'bumf' (in other words, an excess of paperwork, sales brochures or manuscripts from aspirant authors) but how many of us – especially those of a morally-upright character – know what we are really referring to is short for 'bum fodder'? For several centuries, this little phrase was an apt description for trashy literature, and also a term used to describe what we call lavatory paper. So be careful next time you describe something as 'bumf', in case a listener realises the full extent of the insult! Similarly, you should be cautious when calling someone a 'pratt'. After all, how would *you* like to be called a 'buttock' (its real meaning)?

Another word which doesn't sound at all like either 'bum' or 'arse', is the slang word 'jacksy' (also jaxie, jacksie and jacksey-pardy) which was first recorded in the 1896 edition of Farmer & Henley's book *Slang*. The meaning is, of course, 'arse', 'backside' or 'posterior' and the word has cropped up again and again well into modern times. Keith Waterhouse used 'jacksy' in his famous work *Billy Liar* and the word was discussed in *The Sunday Times* (15 September 1963) in respect of Tonbridge boys who said 'a root on the jaxie' for 'a kick in the pants'. So this rather delightful word continues, springing up at regular intervals in poetry and literature, to the present day.

The point is this – there seems to be no aspect of human endeavour which can be safely presumed to be free from invasion by bottom-words. It is, perhaps, their revenge for our inconstancy and fickleness towards them. In Britain, the Milk Marketing Board recently spent millions of pounds telling the public to 'get some bottle'. In all probability, the word 'arse' never crossed the minds of those who devised the advertising campaign. Yet if they had only dug a little deeper . . . They would have found that 'bottle' (colloquially meaning guts or courage) was, in reality, Cockney rhyming slang – 'bottle and glass'. And what does 'glass' rhyme with? You've guessed it.

'Bottle and glass' originally meant 'arse', in the sense of 'bottom' – or weight. A ship's bottom is the part used for freight, stowage and ballast – it helps the ship to keep its centre of gravity on stormy seas. A person with 'bottom', therefore, was a person of guts or gravitas. On the other hand, if you lost your nerve, Cockney rhyming slang would declare that you'd 'lost your bottle', or 'bottled out'. The real meaning is only clear to those in the know – which presumably didn't include the Milk Marketing Board.

Big Sisters of the Breasts

The poet Paul Verlaine, quoted at the beginning of this chapter, was one of the first people to eulogise upon the similarity that buttocks bear to breasts. Subsequently, anthropologists concluded that, in humans as in other primates, the bottom was the original turn-on, and that a pair of fleshy, hemispherical buttocks swung to just the right angle would signal sexual readiness in the female. This, apparently, worked quite well for thousands of years. Then the female of our species decided she preferred to face her lover; perhaps because an upright walking posture slightly changed the position of certain internal organs, and the chances of successful fertilisation became more likely if intercourse occurred from the front. The major problem with this position, of course, was that the buttocks were now entirely hidden from view. So evolution seemed to differentially favour those females who *both* adopted a supine position *and* were able to produce secondary sexual characteristics which would mimic the sexually-stimulating effect of the bottom. This is how a duplicate set of buttocks – better known as breasts – are thought to have acquired such prominence and remarkable sexual significance in the human primate.

It seems, then, that admirers of the female form are getting the best of two evolutionary phases. And what of those amongst us who find themselves more attracted to the posterior portions? Are they some weird throwback from another millenium? Some perverse, animalistic creature lost in the wake of human progress? Not entirely (although some of them may be a bit borderline). Such people are, of course, guardians of a most basic and sustaining aspect of human physical attractiveness. Without people such as these the CanCan and the Black Bottom would never have emerged on to dance floors. Without them the fine Greek and Roman statues standing proudly divested in our museums would have been, instead, deep-relief carvings where every figure had his or her backside pressed firmly, and invisibly, into the wall. Without such ancestral appreciators of the aft anatomy, the whole course of human history would have taken a significantly different turn. As it is, we have a long and salacious history of fondness for the trembling flesh, for thighs like 'two crystal skies' and buttocks, 'those two ambitious hills' (Robert Herrick 1591–1674) that spread and swell to awesome proportions.

Bottoms came into fashion very early in our human history. As soon as we came down out of the trees, so to speak, we began to notice differences between ourselves and our genetic near-neighbours. We saw the male baboon, for instance, present his rear to the dominant male of the group to show subordination while, by this time, most human primates preferred to meet in frontal combat or, indeed, conjugation. And though body painting was very much the vogue, few humans of the time aspired to the fluorescent coloured bottoms of the gibbon. No, the buttocks of our fellow primates must, at that time, have seemed rather vapid affairs – little more than continuations of their sturdy and reliable thighs. We humans, on the other hand, had developed a particularly prominent posterior. As soon as we began to stand, to become bipedal, the shape and set of our skeleton altered in fundamental ways. The pelvis became more compact, in men especially, to enable efficient walking and running. And accompanying that change was a shift in the position, use and strength of the three muscles which form the buttock: the gluteus maximus, gluteus minimus and gluteus medius. These muscles bonded and lifted to become the proud and prominent hemispheres of the modern buttock.

As we shambled our way across the savannah, gathering food and performing other skills of survival, we experienced the simple joy of watching the pert gluteals of the person in front. How comforting it must have been: the rhythmic rise and fall of first one buttock, then the other; the reliable creasing of flesh on each stride forward. And later, in the darkness, nestling into these same plump cushions must have created a deep sense of security and intimacy which sustained us through fear and night terrors. A new body, an emerging new way of life, a growing sense of bond and kinship: the bottom held an important role in all these aspects of early human development.

There is no doubt, too, that the bottom was crucial to the development of religious ritual among our ancestors. One look at the steatopygous (large buttocked) figurines of women unearthed across much of the European continent proves that buttocks were, indeed, an essential feature of our ancestors' equivalent of the Sunday morning church service (perhaps this is the answer to present-day falling church attendances). These clay, wooden or stone figurines are today commonly called 'fertility cult symbols' or 'Venus figurines' in an attempt to explain their very exaggerated depiction of the female form: breasts, stomach and buttocks are all, to put it modestly, of truly gargantuan dimensions. Of course, it is easy to laugh at these forms, to comment, 'Oh, yes, I know a woman like that', or to exclaim 'If that was their idea of beauty, it's a wonder any of us are still here!' But there is another way to view the matter. These figurines were an expression of something deeply meaningful to the people who made them. If we then interpret them only as lust-driven depictions of bigness or three-dimensional pictures of the local beauty queen, we grossly misunderstand the past – and handicap our assessment of the present. No, the Venus figurines, the wall-paintings and stone carvings, are sending us a much more important message.

A clue comes from two goddesses who, though emerging from separate cultures, summarise the depth of meaning and explain the conceptual significance of the big-bottomed figurines. These two goddesses were Gaea (also called Gaia), from the primitive Greek culture, and Isis, from the Egyptian culture. Both were goddesses of fertility. Gaea was a truly immense woman who gave birth to all other deities and also to the first mortals. She was, in fact, called the Earth Goddess or Earth Mother and all life stemmed from her. Now in those days, 'life stemming from' had none of the rather sterile, pious insinuations that it holds today. It meant that all life emerged from her loins, in a very physical and sexual way. Gaea was therefore depicted as fecund and had among her many physical characteristics, a huge bottom.

The second goddess was named Isis and it is important to realise that the meaning of this word 'Isis' is 'seat'. Isis was also a goddess of fertility, a mother goddess. She, too, gave birth to all the life around her and she, also, is represented as having a boundless capacity for giving life. Representations of Isis are less extreme in the physical sense (she did have the head of a cow, but that's another story) than those of Gaea, their only link between their mutual status as earth or mother goddess. Gaea flaunts her status by sheer size, Isis by naming herself the seat of all life. This last image, that of the seat of life, is a timeless image, frequently depicted in pictorial form by, quite literally, seating the mother goddess on the earth. Thus mother and earth unite as one, the seated mother's buttocks spreading to merge with and cover the earth in voluptuous folds of flesh.

Another essential image emerges from this union, one which brings us closer, perhaps, to understanding a further fundamental attraction of buttocks. A woman naturally spreads in girth when she sits until her thighs and buttocks become a lap. She herself becomes a seat. Now she is not only the 'seat' of all life, she is also the soft, hallowed lap that understands and protects all life. Every small human being who has ever curled up in one knows the allure of the lap. Of course, the early Greek and Egyptian cultures were not the only peoples to worship the Great Mother. Virtually every early civilisation had their own version of this goddess and, interestingly, they concurred in the style of their representation of her. That is, she was always amply proportioned, particularly so in the bottom.

So buttocks, and their depiction, were full of appeal and meaning. To early humans, they signalled a difference between themselves and other primates, they provided soft pleasure and intimacy. Buttocks symbolised fecundity as well as the living union between people and planet; this fertile union was all-important as it promised human dominion and successful population. Buttocks *meant* all these things, but they also became – in both fact and symbol – the assurance of comfort, security, protection and warmth.

The Golden Age of the Bottom

By the time of the Roman and later Greek civilisations, the Earth Mother goddess had become the goddess of fertility or the goddess of love. So, in Rome, there is Venus and in Greece Aphrodite, though both were, in fact, the same goddess. Both goddesses had slimmed down considerably since their early, steatopygous days as Earth Mothers. Yet both also drew emphasis to the bottom. Aphrodite (Kallipygos), for instance, was called 'the Fair-Buttocked' and had a temple erected in honour of this particular aspect of her beauty, caused, according to the Greek diarist, Athenaeus, by the following series of events:

The Challenge of the Fair-Buttocked Daughters

A farmer had two beautiful daughters who once fell into a dispute with one another, and even went out on the highway to settle the question which of them had the more beautiful buttocks. One day a youth passed whose father was a rich old man, and to him they displayed themselves; and he, after gazing at them, decided in favour of the older girl; in fact he fell in love with her so passionately that when he returned to town he went to bed ill, and related what had happened to his brother, who was younger than he. So the latter also went into the country to gaze at the girls, and he too fell in love, but with the other girl. Now, the father, at least, begged them to contract a more respectable marriage, but since he failed to persuade them, he brought the girls from their country home to his sons, having got the consent of the girls' father, and joined them in marriage to them. The girls, therefore, were called 'the fair-buttocked' by the townspeople, as Cercidas of Megalopolis relates in his Iambic verses. He says: 'there was a pair of fair-buttocked sisters in Syracuse'. It was they, therefore, who, having come into the possession of splendid wealth, founded the temple of Aphrodite, calling the goddess 'the Fair-buttocked' as related also by Archelaus.

While these sculptures and paintings of Venus/Aphrodite, portrayed naked and in an attitude of confident display, are still here for us to study and gaze upon, the people who devised them and who truly understood their meaning are long since gone. We have little enough information to help us know these people and glimpse their view of the world. But it is clear that these peoples were, collectively, deeply appreciative of life and in particular, beautiful life (little wonder, considering they rarely enjoyed more than three decades of it). Their response was to continuously celebrate life and the body. Athleticism was one way in which celebration and appreciation of the body were combined. Nudity, or tantalising near-nudity, was the norm as athletes of both sexes paraded in front of enthusiastic audiences. Then, in the sweaty grapples or races that followed, no visual delight was forbidden: the entire body was revealed as it moved and struggle and rested. It is necessary, once again, to realise that the bottom had a meaning additional to its anatomical one. The fact that it was so flaunted and so readily available for visual and tactile pleasure symbolised a number of qualities about those cultures, and epitomises the attitude of lusty celebration felt for life and the human body. It indicates a sense of confidence and ease with their existence: they had built fine cities, devised workable social orders and created wealth. They had, surely, earned their pleasures.

So the Etruscans and the Greeks enjoyed nudity and sexual freedom which presented itself both as lust and as worship. The Romans, too, enjoyed sexual freedom but, by that time, nudity was less common and sexual freedom had taken on an air of debauchery. No matter, for these cultures showed agreement in one very important aspect of their view of the world: that physical beauty could represent spiritual wholesomeness. This meant that their appreciation of carnal delights could be justified by, and was in part inspired by, their quest for moral quality. Their delight in a youthful bottom – strong, firm and smooth – was a partial expression of the new and deeper delight with an emerging all-encompassing morality.

On the other side of the world, remains of Sanskrit texts indicate that other cultures were also seeking to integrate the physical, mental and spiritual dimensions of life into one coherent philosophy. Old Sanskrit texts defining ideals of feminine beauty proclaim that, amongst other attributes, the woman should have 'heavy hips' and that her 'loins have large buttocks'.

The ancient Egyptians also practised a bit of tattooing, which is the introduction of pigments through punctures in the skin, and included the bottom in their handiwork. It is likely, though not certain, that tattooing the tush was for semi-erotic purposes in ancient Egypt. Not so in other tattooing or scarring (cicatrisation) cultures. The Oceanic cultures, such as the Maori of New Zealand, the Eskimos, Japanese and some African tribes decorated the buttocks with patterns that meant something far more than 'hey, look at *my* bottom!' Their designs were often complex, such as the Maori's spirals, and usually indicated good breeding and an understanding of, or a quest for, a wholistic vision of life. These patterns were displayed on the bottom and often repeated on the subject's face. Obviously, there was no flippancy or lewdness here but an attempt to express the integration of body with the inner and spiritual worlds.

The Great Cover-Up

Throughout the Middle Ages, European men and women followed the fluctuations of fashion with enthusiasm, expending great effort in order to clothe themselves in the latest styles. In fact, men were rather more responsive to the dictates of fashion than were women. They took every opportunity to emphasise the part of the body currently in favour, clothing themselves in styles that shifted to emphasise the shoulders, legs, chest, genitals and, of course, the buttocks. A great deal of wadding and padding was employed during this period because, as is so often the case with fashions in clothing, once one person exaggerates a part of the anatomy, everyone who wishes to keep in vogue must follow suit. There is no strong indication as to why the changes in male fashion should have taken place so often and so significantly (why does it today?) although we may surmise that they were governed, at least in part, by the attentions of women.

Prior to about 1760, men were as interested in clothing their bodies in an alluring and fashionable manner as are the women of today. But around 1760 men began, suddenly it seemed, to adopt a fairly uniform style of dress which ignored changes in fashion. Historians differ as to their explanations of this change. Most agree that male dress, at this time, became hierarchical – that it served to establish status and socio-economic position rather than simply to attract attention from the opposite sex. Other historians believe that at this time men decided to take the upper hand in the 'war of the sexes' and, using the power created by their subdued manner of dress, demanded that women play the more passive (and more decorated) role of 'object to be looked at'. This implies that men no longer expressed a need to be viewed but, rather, a need to view and to exercise power by granting acceptance or rejection of what they saw. Whether or not this is the case, towards the end of the eighteenth century, women became the main focus of changes in fashion and, while various parts of the female anatomy were chosen for emphasis over the following decades, men most definitely took on the role of observer and, increasingly, the role of the 'active' sex. This era marks a very strange and important occasion in socio-sexual history. Not only were the male and female posteriors given different values, they were both sublimated to re-emerge into socio-sexual practices of a somewhat perverse nature, as we shall see.

One historian has suggested that fashion and the ideals of female beauty established at this time produced women who were actually caricatures of the female body. They were corsetted and laced and bound and draped according to the particular extreme or exaggerated definition of 'female' currently in use. Of course, some women were more willing than others to be moulded in this way, but the enduring impression of this age is one of S-shaped women with minuscule waists and rather weighty bosoms and derrières. Their centres of gravity must have shifted tremendously from the norm, and the health of their lumbar vertebrae must have suffered considerably.

By the nineteenth century, women were well used to displaying themselves – insofar as decency allowed – to the less fashionable but more dynamic male. And in their unspoken attempts at attracting the agreeable gaze of any passing male, female fashion in clothing and body shape continued to shift, emphasising first one part of the body, then another. The bottom had its turn, of course, and enjoyed a very long period of popularity.

What did this popularity consist of? You will remember that our early ancestors were attracted to one another's bottoms because they had *meaning*. They were symbols of comfort, kinship and one's status as a human being. By the time of fashionable European ladies promenading in the parks, however, these symbols had settled into the dust of a dim subconscious. The nineteenth century was a time when Europe was endeavouring to lift itself into a state of affluent refinement. Such a formidable purpose as that requires all the focus and attention a society is able to give, leaving little time for the sweaty games and wholesale eroticism available to the Greeks and Etruscans. No, during this time of industrialisation and the generation of wealth, sex and everything concerned with it went underground. The bottom was hidden away and treated as a coarse, even primitive aspect of human nature and anatomy. It no longer had meaning by the fact of its being available; rather, it had meaning because it was *not* available. Whereas their forebears could smack or stroke a passing bottom with ease (and little forethought), Europeans of the eighteenth and nineteenth centuries placed the bottom on a dark and forbidden pedestal, to be attained only after a long and tortuous journey through social propriety and many frustrating layers of cloth. The bottom could be seen as a vestige of what we feared and suspected was our suppressed animality, later to be uncloaked by the likes of Darwin and Freud. The brazen, semi-lustrous globe, once contemptuously displayed in full public view, now pouted in tenebrous isolation.

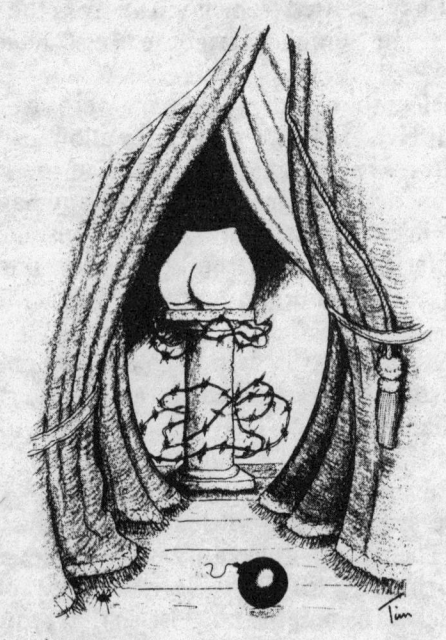

On a Dark and Forbidden Pedestal

Perhaps the hidden, coveted bottom of these times performed a very necessary task, however. For it is widely accepted that secrecy breeds curiosity, and there is little more stimulating to the libido than curiosity and an anticipation of revelation. Paradoxically, this era of repressed sexuality gave rise to an extraordinary amount of pornographic literature and whore-houses. It seems likely that few men were ultimately deprived of sexual satisfaction and that, en route to their pleasures, they encountered the bottom. What we don't know for certain is whether the bottom was displayed in its full glory during such encounters, or simply grappled with in the semi-darkness of those layers of cloth already mentioned.

During Victorian times, the bosom, neck and shoulders were the most flaunted erogenous zones (plus occasional flirtations with the erotic ankle). The bottom grew larger and more dimpled during this era. Few bottoms had the elegant athleticism of the early bottom, or the ruddy complexion of the Rubens variety. Hugeness was the norm and was poetically described as plump, full-bodied, rounded or even rotund! In fact, plumpness was actively desired and the anonymous author of *My Secret Life*, a supposedly autobiographical account of various erotic encounters, tell us that 'a small foot, a round, plump leg and thigh and a fat backside speak to the prick straight', and emphasises the point by going on to assert that 'few men will keep long to a bony lady whose skinny buttocks can be held in one hand'.

Refined and sophisticated as they were, the Victorians were still greatly enamoured of fecundity and the promise of 'Nutritive Beauty', in the phrase of one Victorian who compiled a major study on female attractiveness. They saw women as, primarily, mothers and objects of sexual desire. Any other attributes, such as intelligence, were considered a bonus or, to some, a nuisance which could undermine the woman's intended function in life. Where, precisely, the bottom began and ended is of somewhat less importance in this era than in the times before and since. For to have got as far as the bottom was, in most senses, to have arrived. It would therefore be of little concern whether the bottom hung from the scaffolding of the pelvis or climbed effortlessly to adjoin the waist. Either, once discovered, presaged the events and intimacies of the next few minutes or hours – most likely, one feels, to have been minutes.

It goes without saying that there was no social tolerance of nudity during this time. In fact, it may be argued that nudity would have undermined the lusty enjoyment of surreptitious peeks and glimpses, so often written of in literature of the time.

People throughout history have known that a little clothing can heighten the appeal of a lot of flesh, whereas a lot of flesh without any clothing can overwhelm the senses and all but curtail one's pleasure.

As sex and sensuality were driven further and further underground by the prudish values of those times, displacement activities began to occur. We begin to find symbols of sex in hitherto obscure, even inanimate, places. Chairs and tables, for instance, were dressed in frilly skirts to hide their legs for fear that, seeing them, visiting gentlemen would be overcome with passionate desire. One hopes their desire was for human rather than furniturial company (perhaps the aberrant desires of today's poodles and other small dogs could be curbed by this strategy). Certainly, the language at the time was amended so that women had 'limbs' rather than 'legs' but, all in all, the sensitivity displayed in these matters seems uncomfortably false. On the principle of it being impossible to make a silk purse out of a sow's ear, it seems unlikely that the very base attitudes of the time could be so easily rectified by a little verbal circumlocution.

One look at the fashion in women's clothing will illustrate the point. On the surface the women appear flounced and flowered and 'too good to touch' – the long neck and soft shoulders, the powder-puff cleavage and pasty-white upper arms. Further down the body, all is hidden in metres of gathered and pleated cloth. The effect, and indeed the purpose, was to enhance the image of steatopygous woman, at once exerting powerful, mysterious appeal while at the same time enforcing a most definite taboo. The bows and bustles and huge, swaying skirt of a woman clothed in this way invited the observer to associate her with all of his pre-conditioned ideas of womanhood but forbade him to observe or sense the reality. He was encouraged to remain buttock-conscious by the overstated derrières in women's fashion, yet prevented from gaining a true understanding of the buttock in its natural form.

Of course, there were ample opportunities for men to gaze upon, fondle or otherwise engage with the fleshy protuberances. The nineteenth century harboured a booming trade in obscene, lewd and smutty literature and illustration.

In major cities, whole streets became famous for this sort of merchandising, co-existing with the more active form, that of prostitution. Classic pieces of literature and art were reproduced in bawdy style to lessen the guilt of prospective purchasers, and also to sidestep the lengthening arm of the law. Even the technology of the time was entrusted with the fine art of titillation. Photography developed to the point where it was easy and inexpensive to devote whole shops to pornographic pictures. In addition, the stereoscope, an invention of Wheatstone and Brewster, gave an added dimension of reality – or unreality – to the quest for sexual satisfaction through arousing images.

Significant to these times was an increase in the popularity of spanking. Some brothels specialised in spanking, employing women and young boys adept at both giving and receiving the blows. And the literature, photography and illustration of this genre was full of plump-bottomed women folded over the knees of authoritative looking men. Just occasionally, and probably commanding a greater price, there were illustrations of role reversals where a robust and matronly woman was depicted landing some smart spanks to the rear of an eminent male creature, such as a judge, vicar or politician. Here, at least, the bottom was the sole object of attention and the man could briefly gain reprieve from his self-inflicted role of the 'active' and 'powerful' male.

So it went for a great many decades. Mores evolved into great, immovable monoliths while fashion flirted with the attentions and sensibilities of men and women alike. One very controversial and, for many, enjoyable development was the appearance of the crinoline – the voluminous dress thrown over a metal hoop-skirt which was worn in mid-Victorian times (and later developed into the bustle). Crinolines were renowned for causing the ankles, 'limbs' or even the bottom to be displayed when the hoop performed one of its unexpected sweeping or lifting movements. This obviously caused considerable excitement, but – just imagine – crinolines also enabled women to wear little or nothing underneath their skirts! In 1853 the Kensington Petty Sessions recorded the case of a Mrs Lowe, of Victoria Grove, who permitted her servant girl to 'stand on the sill of an upstairs window, in order to clean it, whereby the life of the servant was endangered and the public decency shocked'. Mrs Lowe was, as a result of this incident, charged under some law or other, though whether she was ever convicted is unclear. The shock to public decency was caused by the fact that the servant girl was wearing a crinoline and *only* a crinoline. The gentleman who informed on Mrs Lowe and her servant must have relished his total and uncompromising view before he, very priggishly, made his way to the courts to lay charges.

Later, in the 1870s, the bustle came once more into vogue, as the erogenous zone shifted from bosoms to bellies to bottoms. The effect was one of exaggeration, which the bustle created in both the front and back of the body. Once again, the shameless use of copious padding and wadding was employed to achieve the desired curves, although many beauty writers of the day discouraged this practice. The bustle was most definitely a celebration of the derrière. In its exaggerated silhouette one can see the form of those steatopygous women of Paleolithic times who seem to have such a profound effect on our instincts. The bustle not only gave every woman that same primal form, it enabled every woman to accentuate and redeem what she could of her physical characteristics so that she could enjoy being beautiful, in the particular notion of beauty then prevailing. Which brings us, briefly, back into the parks to see the corsetted women swaying and swishing their promenade. You might, understandably, exclaim 'How awful!' but wait just a moment. As the women walked, the bustle produced a wagging motion which not only exaggerated their mincing grace but was, to some extent, a turn-on for them. And if we look at some of the erotic photographs of the time we see that some of these rather chunky pin-ups readily assume this 'bustle pose'; that is, they thrust their bottoms up and back and their breasts up and forward. The result: an exaggerated curve of the spine into a position of sexual readiness which has been familiar to humans for . . . well, as long as there have been humans.

But we can't leave this most fascinating and contradictory time without paying a compliment to the unknown creators of the CanCan, the dance that outraged Paris in the 1830s, London in 1867 and then much of Europe before the killjoys swept it from the stages in the mid-1870s. The CanCan consisted of orgasmic rhythms, fast and aggressive movements, and, of course, ecstatic high kicks which thrilled audiences and threw the dancers into a frenzy of steamy, throbbing pleasure. It was first performed in London on Boxing Day, 1867, by one Josephine Durwend, also known as Finette, and was immortalised in musical terms by Jacques Offenbach in *Orpheus in the Underworld*. The dance is, of course, essentially a bottom-dance, and what it has done for the appreciation and the wider exhibition of the bottom is without doubt immeasurable. Although high-kicking such as that done in the CanCan is an ingredient of many dances, most associated with fertility rites, it is likely that Europe had never seen its equal within living memory. Naturally, the sensibilities of all right-thinking people were outraged – and stimulated, too. The genuine dance (as opposed to Hollywood's covered-up version) enabled the audience to see the whole business: limbs, thighs, buttocks and the hitherto hidden meeting place of these massively taboo features. The display was joyful, raucous, unrestrained; the reception was unconditionally enthusiastic. For bottoms and bottom-lovers of the time, The CanCan was an exploration of virgin territory, and a celebration of their arrival at a place which had formerly been strictly and puritanically forbidden.

The New Tolerance

As the twentieth century dawned and the monarch changed from Victoria to Edward, so the fashion in bodies and clothing changed too. The extreme S-shape resolved to a more natural (or at least a less pronounced) S-shape as women lost their grotesquely huge hoops and bustles. The bottom became the feature of the day and a middle-ground was struck, in terms of size, by ignoring both the bustle and the real bottom in favour of simple padding. The bosom was taken down a notch or two also and became a less prominent mono-bosom: a relatively demure shelf of flesh that served to add emphasis to the bottom. Some historians would disagree with this interpretation of the era, claiming instead that the bust was the main attraction, not the bottom. But it rather depends on your point of view. Let us examine some insights into the Edwardian vision of the bottom. To begin with, the male bottom began to emerge again, after a long period of atrophy. Trousers suddenly seemed to show off what had previously been tidied away under loose trews and long coats and the growing interest in sea swimming created new and more revealing designs in men's swimwear. Even the language of the time relaxed to include references to the gluteal orbs. 'Kiss my arse' re-emerged into common usage at this time, harking back to a much earlier time and a far more serious usage.

Further, the Edwardian fascination with the bottom continued to popularise the art of spanking as a semi-sadistic, erotic act – frequently depicted in photograph, illustration and stereoscopic form. Many brothels of the time specialised in spanking; both men and women could attend and express their whims on both male and female buttocks. In fact, so ingrained had the concept and practice of spanking become, especially in the wealthier classes, that a very great proportion of men used this practice as a means of reiterating their dominant, masculine role within their own households. There are no records of how women of the time responded to this demeaning and rather prurient charade. However, it is worth noting that other unusual forms of behaviour were also becoming more prevalent. Frotteurism, for instance (in which a man brings his pleasure to a climax against the clothed bottom of a woman) occurred more than infrequently in the stairways and corridors of the well-housed rich and influential. This act, usually perpetrated by the gentlemen residents upon the servant girls and women, did little physical harm yet introduced a stain of obscenity into an otherwise natural desire to make contact.

One should not be too surprised, perhaps, that behaviour such as frotteurism and wholesale spanking became commonplace. For men had sublimated their desires and attractions for 150 years in an attempt to bring about change of one sort or another. Perhaps they succeeded; certainly the cost in socio-sexual terms was very high indeed as it is almost certainly this time which hatched many of the diseases of sexual cruelty and perversity which are with us to this day.

When World War One broke out in Europe, fashion in both clothing and anatomical preference was frozen in time. Young men went off to war and left their sweethearts in fluffy, curvaceous anticipation of their return. But the impact of war honed the fluffiness into a more severe, but more natural, female shape and the bottom often all but disappeared under mourning gowns and austerity designs. Then, after the war was over, the male bottom and the female ankle jostled for shock-value in the drawing rooms and dance halls of Europe and America. In the 1920s, men, perhaps relaxed after their years in service enduring the hot breath of death on their necks, resumed some of the romantic poses and physiques not enjoyed by men since the seventeenth century. They danced by wiggling their hips, and therefore their bottoms. They wore trousers that did not confine their anatomy and they had lewd, rude parties that frequently included nude bathing, debagging and very chummy physical relationships. Women loved it. Their dresses showed (at the very least) their ankles, and much more if they could – climbing ever higher in tassles and trims until the skirts became properly mini: sometimes five inches above the knee! But what about those dresses? They flattened the bosom, ignored the waist and treated the hips, pelvis and buttocks as one. And the dresses tantalised the line of leg and thigh with startling splits that often climbed right over the hip. To complete the picture, stockings were lengthened to rise not just over the knee (all that was necessary earlier), but well beyond the thigh. Place all of that on the dance floor with those jazzed up men, set them both wriggling and gyrating and you have a recipe for revolution.

Well, there nearly was one. But the Great Depression happened instead. A little less flamboyant, perhaps, but the ankles and bottoms held their ground and writhed their way through poverty and calamity as though they provided some sort of salve for the suffering. For both men and women the bottom was freer than it had been for a long time with little in the way of clothing or corsetry to contain or restrain it. Skirts stayed well above the ankle and, for the first time ever, it became fashionable for women to wear shorts and trousers. The natural bottom was back!

Stepping Out, Turning Out

The thrilling revelation that women had two buttocks, the same as men and that they were ready and willing to show them happened just in time for World War Two. Men were marched off to war, again, and were sent copies of that famous Betty Grable poster later, when the war suddenly became long and serious. Betty appeared in a swimsuit, peering coyly over one shoulder, her buttocks vying for attention with the look of promise in her eyes. No sylph-like demoiselle, Betty and all those who emulated her were *real* women with haunches you could get hold of. Men needed women like this to give purpose to their lives . . . So the fashion editors said, anyway. And so it had been during every other warring period in our history, the bottom becoming more fleshy and more socially prominent during periods of widespread aggression.

But when there is fighting there is invariably flaunting. Europe a few decades earlier had ruptured its seams at the shock of the CanCan; now America and Europe swooned at the new and outrageous display of tightly knickered bottoms in the dance-halls performing dances such as the Jitterbug, the Black Bottom and the Jive. Every movement of the gluteal formation that could be incurred, was incurred, and anyone who could stand the impact was free to watch or join in. The pace was breathless, the rhythm irresistible, the outcome raunchy and totally refreshing. With such a rousing and reckless expenditure of energy, who could help but put the worries and fears of war and poverty aside?

When the war ended, the hardy derrières lost none of their breadth, only softened to become the housewives and baby-boomers of the 1950s. Their ampleness smiled out of two-piece swimsuits and stretched the seams of the all new pedal-pushers. In fact, the 1950s became the most bottom-conscious period since the Edwardian era. Fashion worshipped the bottom, whether male or female, and pulled out all the stops to create bottom-enhancing styles. So, apart from those swimming suits and pedal-pushers, the haunch-hugging sweater dress was born and later, for men, those 'bun-hugging' trousers so often worn by the rock 'n' rollers of the time.

This period also produced one of the most famous bottoms of all time, that of Marilyn Monroe. She was somehow able to bring a special quality of beauty to the bottom for, no matter what she wore, she carried hers with pride and a distinct, provocative charm. Women of the time did their best to imitate her, which certainly helped to keep the bottom 'tops' as far as fashion, beauty and men were concerned. Certainly, since this time, the bottom has never been totally out of the social limelight.

The 1960s and '70s fairly ran amok with the bottom, and the rest of the body, too, it must be said. Apart from a fairly brief flirtation with such monstrosities as the tent dress, the shirt dress and the smock, fashion treated the body as though it had only just been discovered and did its best to outline all of its salient features. So the mini-skirt, hot-pants and the bikini encased (but only just) the untamed bottoms of women and girls throughout Europe, America and Japan. And men kept their blue jeans tight across their rumps, although the cut of leg changed from stove-pipe to bell-bottomed and back again.

Strangely enough, with so much revelation going on there seemed very little meaning assigned to the rear anatomy, very little inner revelation, in fact. There were loud murmurings of 'free love', 'getting rid of hang-ups' and 'finding yourself' but these actually did little to draw attention or give value to the bottom. Instead, the bottom seemed merely one of three or four physical hooks on which to hang the latest cultural statement. There is certainly nothing wrong in this, it is just that it comes as something of a disappointment after the altogether more genteel and promising '50s bottoms.

Then, in the late '70s, *The Sunday Times* newspaper, in Britain, conducted a survey to determine which areas of men's bodies women found most attractive. To understand why this survey was conducted, one must remember that a long period of 'unisex' fashions had broken down many of the socio-sexual expectations and visual stimuli to which both men and women had become so accustomed. Further, women were writing and talking freely and publicly about orgasm, female satisfaction and their own sexual needs. From the public reaction which ensued, it seems likely that men, and perhaps women too, had never heard of such things and didn't know what to do with them now that they *had* heard of them! It is also almost certain that men began to suffer from confusion, doubt and loss of self-confidence within the male/female arena.

The Sunday Times survey proved to be one of the first of many such attempts at revealing what women wanted, what they thought and how men stood, after all, in the sexual battlefield (for battlefield it had become). The survey showed that men imagined women were most attracted to them according to their muscular chest and shoulders, muscular arms, penis, height, flat stomach, slimness, hair texture, buttocks, eyes, long legs and neck. In that order. But – surprise, surprise – women didn't reveal the same set of priorities in their assessment of a man's attractiveness. In the survey, women named a man's most important features in this order: buttocks, slimness, flat stomach, eyes, long legs, height, hair, neck, penis, muscular chest and shoulders, muscular arms. So, a trying two hundred years after men had put the dampers on involving themselves in fashion, they were enticed back into the fray by a very clear statement – such as was indicated in the survey – that women liked their bottoms!

As the 1980s dawned in tentative sobriety, a bright beacon of hope shone through the mists of socio-sexual restlessness and confusion: the bottom was back. Surveys, such as that just mentioned, became a commonplace feature in glossy magazines and dailies. Books were published on the care and exercise of the bottom; sweaty classes were held in aromatic gymnasia where bottoms were bashed and bounced to whip them into 'shape'. For the bottom had suddenly become athletic. No 'love handles' and dimpled delights for the '80s man or woman, just firm, supple litheness which would guarantee a pinch at the next office party. An article printed in *Today* newspaper in 1987 talked of *women* sex pests, claiming that men as well as women were the victims of bottom pinching and sexy sniggers at work. A NUPE health union official apparently had to deal with embarrassed young men who were accosted in hospital wards by 'old' ladies who rubbed up against them!

The bottom is back and there is a great deal of value and meaning attached to it. For a start, it has commercial clout. A blue jeans manufacturer named popular actress Felicity Kendal the 'Rear of the Year' in 1981 and did a roaring trade. And pictures of pert peaches appear frequently in parent and childcare magazines proclaiming 'babycare starts at the bottom' and other such platitudes. Throughout the '80s the bottom has held an important aesthetic niche in the hearts and minds of men and women alike. It has become more beautiful than its recent forebears, of that there is no doubt, and has come to symbolise commitment to a certain lifestyle as a result. In this respect, the late twentieth century bottom most closely resembles those of the ancient Greeks and Etruscans. For today's beautiful bottom is well-nourished, well-exercised, well-sunned and much-loved. There are very few signs of embarrassment or inhibition currently associated with the bottom, but quite a few indications that it is becoming one of the most cherished and revered parts of the body.

Nevertheless, there are some slightly disturbing aspects associated with this late twentieth-century flowering of the bottom. Not least its appearance in weird and quirky 'scientific' experiments called the Brock Pleasure Machine to give 'intensity-graded waves of pleasure' to someone's buttocks! The research claimed to discover that some people like to give other people big pleasure waves while other people like to give some people small pleasure waves. Is that kinky, or what?

Even more depraved are some of the collaborations between the legal and psychiatric professions which have flourished throughout the 70s and 80s. In one instance, a conjoining of law and sexology, an Arizona court decided that lewd and lascivious acts did not always constitute 'unnatural' conduct. The court ruled that rubbing one's penis on a victim's buttocks did not constitute an unnatural act and so was not punishable by law. This is nothing less than good old frotteurism which

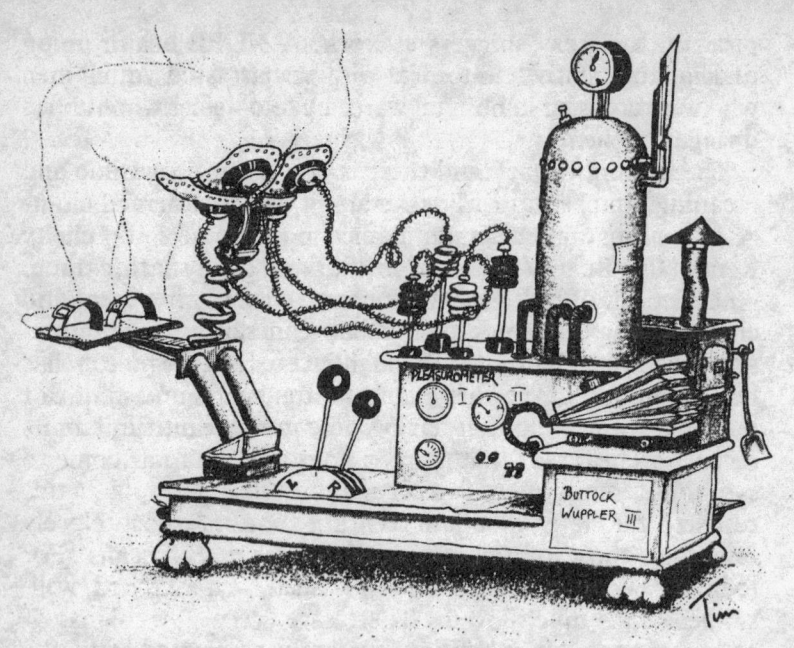

A Prototype Buttock Wuppler

now seems to have become incorporated into the Arizonan constitution.

And not content to laugh along with the rest of the population, one British social worker of questionable sanity explored the activity known as 'mooning', in which the buttocks are exposed to public scrutiny. Interviews were conducted with both 'witnesses and performers' before the social worker decided – no, hypothesised – that 'mooning' is 'an act descriptive of or symbolic of various issues specific to late adolescence', and . . . 'an attempt to place the origin of these issues within the anal phase'. Come again?

So, while the end of the twentieth century might be a time of 'you've never had it so good' for the bottom, we still have further to go before we can free ourselves from the past centuries of cluneal restraint. Old thorns keep surfacing. For instance, during the 1989 Oscar ceremonies, one actress rose to claim her award wearing a – wait for it – *bustle*! On the other hand, actress/singer Cher apparently spent $3000 on having her bottom rebuilt – that's one way of accepting middle age. And that bad old Victorian habit, spanking, continues to be very popular: one London restaurant even promises customers a spanking from Matron if they don't finish their meal.

Peaceful or not, the bottom triggers all sorts of thoughts and emotions in both owners and observers. This is as it should be, for the bottom is an essentially human characteristic which will not, for long, lie dormant and untended. But as we leave this brief discussion of the bottom and its history, we must remember above all else that the bottom is here to give us pleasure. It is a rare gift of our development as humans and we must, therefore, accept its blessings and graces with joy.

2

BOTTOM SPOTTING FOR BEGINNERS

Let's divert our attentions to a more practical purpose at this point. As Pierre Charron almost said many centuries ago (well, he would have done if he'd thought about it) 'the proper study of mankind is hams'. As a Rookie Rumpster, you are – no doubt – breathlessly impatient to come to grips, so to speak, with the systematic study of the rear end. History is all very well, but right now, you're itching to get some practical experience, right? Have patience, fellow spotter of bottoms. You enthusiasm is highly commendable, but before you can consider yourself a professional clunologist (from the Latin *clunes* for buttocks) you must learn the craft from one end to the other. Clunology is a scientific discipline which is all about following haunches, not hunches. Remember, the end always justifies the beans. So, with the help of another consenting adult (please note: the experiments described here should be performed by consenting adults only – to do otherwise would be not only illegal, but also a severe insult to the ancient study of clunology and its long and respectable list of proponents), let us begin.

First, you must learn how to assess quickly any candidate bottom according to the ten basic Cluneal Characteristics. Each and every bottom in the world can be categorised into one of the following types. With some practice, you may even become so proficient in this art that the subject of your studies may never realise that he or she has been skilfully appraised and evaluated. But whatever you do, *don't stare!*

The Ten Cluneal Characteristics

1. The Profile

The study of profile must begin with the question Where does the bottom begin? At exactly what point does the thigh swell and rise to become the buttock? Part of our answer must come from a very brief reference to anatomical studies, particularly of the gluteal muscles. For it is these muscles which altered all those years ago to give the human race its first bottom.

Alternatively, we could perform mathematical calculations as to the rate at which the thigh broadens for each centimetre it climbs. It is best, however, to *sense* the bottom; to use your powers of observation to *understand* the character of each and every bottom you observe. To that end, here are five typical examples of bottom profiles, by which you may hone your sensitive eye . . .

The Low-Slung Profile

This bottom appears to begin about half way down the thigh. There are several possible reasons for this phenomenon: ageing and lack of exercise can cause the gluteal muscles to relax so that the bottom sags, an effect which is more pronounced in a very weighty bottom. (For tips on how to prevent this loathsome calamity, please refer to Chapter Three.) However, take heart – some people are naturally low-slung. Their thighs thicken considerably immediately they lift away from the knees and, usually, this is due to their musculature, not fatty tissue. Fine examples may be seen amongst athletes involved in heavyweight sports such as wrestling, shot-putting, javelin throwing and weight-lifting. It is equally common to both men and women, and demands certain special precautions and considerations. For instance, in the 1960s, when the mini-skirt was introduced into high fashion, those women with low-slung derrières were at a decided disadvantage. And in the 1950s and '60s, men with low-slung profiles often found it downright impossible to fit into the drainpipe trousers so fashionable at the time. At its saggy worst, it may appear a bleak, cheerless and sombre spectacle. However, if well-toned, a great number of people find this profile very beautiful, even sexy. For there is an undeniable aura of power and compact sexuality in this gracefully manoeuvred bottom.

Famous historical personage exhibiting a low-slung profile: Alfred Hitchcock, director of *The Rear View Mirror*.

The Tear-Drop Profile

Most commonly, but not exclusively, found on females. It is usually soft, not to say floppy, with the minimum of obvious muscle tone. It is easily observed when the owner is wearing jeans or, if a woman, one of those delightful sweater-dresses that hide almost nothing from the experienced clunologist. As the name indicates, the Tear-Drop bottom concentrates its bulk and weight at the lower aspect of the bottom – so much so that the cheeks actually hang over the thigh somewhat. Often people who are considered 'long-waisted' are simultaneously tear-dropped and, in fact, the one feature enhances the other by creating a very long, sloping line of the back. A tear-drop bottom provides a nice cushion for the owner to sit upon but, to the observer it virtually disappears (in profile at least) when the owner is seated. This creates a most unusual straight-spine effect which is itself an attractive feature, and should provide

the practiced clunologist with a firm indication of the type of profile to expect. The blue-jean, and especially the more recent loose styles, shows off the tear-drop to good advantage in both men and women. Very baggy trousers do absolutely nothing for it, and neither do those very tight pencil-line skirts (they make the tear-drop appear quite ugly and confined). On the other hand, for a woman a French-cut, heavy-knit skirt is extremely flattering to this profile allowing, as it does, a little room for a discreet wobble of the cheeks.
Famous historical personage exhibiting a tear-drop profile: Attila, often called 'the Bun'.

The Hillock Profile

The Hillock is cluneal near-symmetry. The buttocks develop out of the thighs in a graceful, even curve. They rise and gain prominence without any sudden or vulgar changes in curvature, then as gracefully slope up and inwards toward the lower back. The result is a hillock of flesh that sits proud and balanced between two identical curves above and below its apex. It is currently enjoying a period of fashionable chic. Not only do most exercise classes focus much of their time on helping pupils to establish this profile for themselves, but most 'designer' fashions in women's clothing are cut for this profile – and poor you if you haven't got it! Certainly it is a most versatile and attractive profile to own, but it indicates the most atrocious physical fascism to assume that everyone should, and indeed could, have or even want this profile. A great many men sport the hillock profile, especially those who have athletic foibles. It seems likely that men who are especially slim and tall make up the greatest percentage of hillock-profiled people, but studies to confirm or refute this conjecture are still underway.

It usually promises a tight, firm bottom with very little surplus body to promote sway, wobble or bounce. In fashion terms, the hillock looks excellent in Gatsby trousers, swimming skins and tight blue jeans. Women who enjoy the hillock profile are almost without exception athletic or fitness-oriented women. This is not to say that becoming athletic or fitness-oriented will, by itself, produce this profile for you – you can't make a mountain out of a mole-hillock. No, you must have the physical tendency for this profile to start with, and that's down to genetics. Whether by luck or by lather, however, if you end up with a hillock profile, you will look fabulous in skin-tight mini-skirts, tight jeans and jodphurs, swimsuits and probably just about anything else you like on the fashion scene. Lucky you!

Famous historical personages exhibiting a hillock profile:
Rogers and Hammerstein, writers of 'The Hills Are Alive . . . '

The Flat Profile

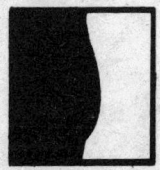

Bloodless and intellectual in appearance, this bland outline leaves some onlookers completely cold, while others are definitely fired and flushed by its effect. As the name applies, this profile is almost a non-profile. For here the buttocks give only the merest hint of being buttocks at all and enjoy a very muted life of their own – sadly, most flat bottomed people have rarely enjoyed a wobble or a sway, for instance. Thin people, both male and female, are the most likely owners of the flat profile and so this characteristic usually suits them. Just occasionally an otherwise sturdily-built person will possess a flat bottom and this can be an unfortunate feature unless cleverly disguised. For instance, the sturdy person with a flat profile bottom should make sure they wear well-fitted clothing

with an emphasis on long jackets, full-cut skirts and closely fitting trousers. Similarly, thin people with this profile should avoid very baggy trousers – which will only augment the flatness of their profile – and clothes, such as hip-hugging skirts and jeans, which rely on a heftier bottom to balance the effect. Provided it is a correctly-managed asset, the flat profiled bottom could be a ticket to fame and fortune, however. A great many male pop-stars have flaunted a flat profile and been mobbed for it! Flat can mean fanciable. Each cheek is usually quite tiny and there are no end of people who go crazy at the thought of holding one cheek in the palm of each hand. So if you're a Flatty, dress for emphasis and use what little you have in a prominent way.
Famous historical personage exhibiting a flat profile: William Pitt, often called 'The Bottomless Pitt'.

The Rising Orb Profile

At its best, this is a most incredible phenomenon to witness. Here, the buttocks seem to have a mind of their own, and there is absolutely nothing subtle about them. They do not rise gracefully out of the thighs, nor do they slope gently from the small of the back. No, the rising orb buttocks seem to erupt from the rear where, rhinoceros-like, they spend the rest of their natural lives riding tremulously on their perch high above the ground. These buttocks may almost be seen as two globes attached to the meeting place of thigh and back. They are fully round, that is to say spherical, and are a nearly equal mixture of muscle and fatty tissue. Their most impressive characteristic is that they are erect – they do not sag or flop or pout but quiver confidently in their immensity. The rising orb profile promises hugeness and unstinting largesse. This is not to say that the

THE TEN TOP TUSHES OF ALL TIME

Brigitte Nielson (tallest), an inspiration to the younger generation.

The proud owner of a 'Rear of the Year' award, Lulu coyly displays her cluneal characteristics, notwithstanding the hot-pants. A rare blend of Peaches (rear view), Hillocks (profile) and Not A Glimmer (sunlight factor).

Sharing strikingly similar cluneal characteristics, and probably purchasing their undergarments from the same mail-order lingerie supplier, Diana Ross and Madonna clearly merit a 'top ten' position together.

Another 'tie' for a 'top ten' position, Marilyn Monroe and Jane Russell.

Although the poet Verlaine described the buttocks as 'big sisters of the breasts', in Samantha Fox's case the relationship may have been interestingly reversed.

Iceman John Curry's bot is so hot that his jété turned into a sauté.

Ed 'Peaches' Moses proving that a fun bum can run some.

Earl T. Bigelow, winner of the Milton Keynes Svelte Sphincter Award, demonstrates his assets.

The traditional seat of the kings and queens of England.

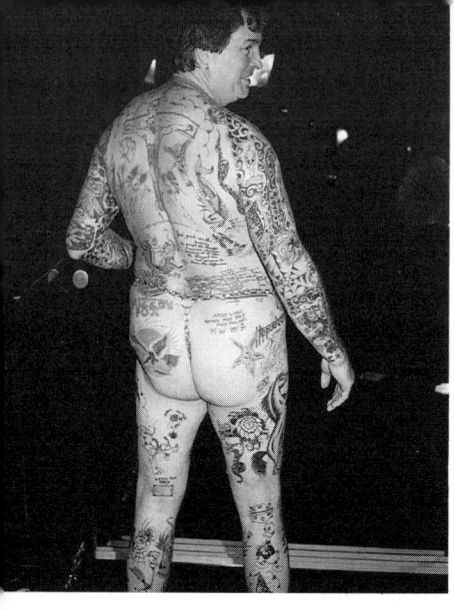

TEN TATTERED, TASTELESS TAILS

Hamish McButt, an aspiring entrant in this year's Edinburgh Tattoo, demonstrates the range and breadth of his repertoire. Why is his rear end so lightly decorated compared to the rest of his anatomy? "I ha' na' found the man to do it justice," says Hamish, "and besides, it costs more for the rear end".

Ronald Reagan trying to find his elbow.

Mohammed Ali proves that it's not what you've got, it's the way that you use it.

Is it a cream cake? Is it a Kiwi fruit? No! It's Elton John's bottom.

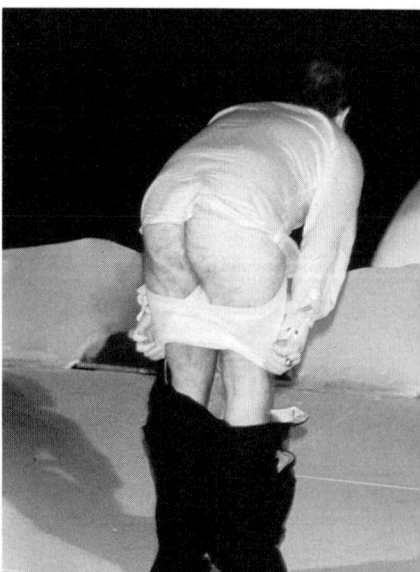

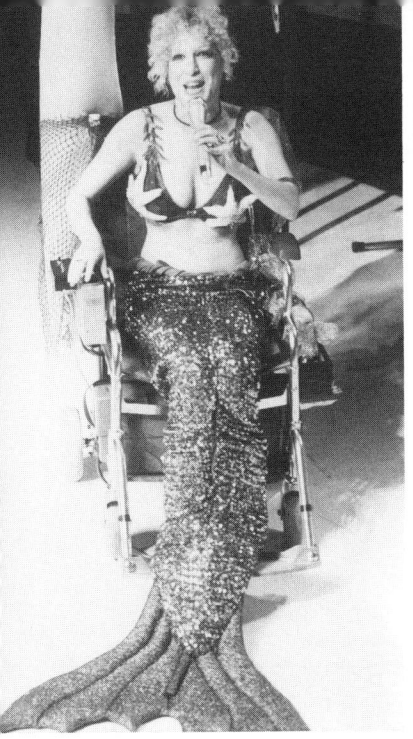

Bette Midler demonstrates a rare phenomenon where the Low Slung profile becomes *so* low that it merges with the knees and when the rear view surpasses Pears and exceeds Bunches of Grapes to become Codfish.

A justifiably anonymous bottom, hopefully receiving some expert salvage advice.

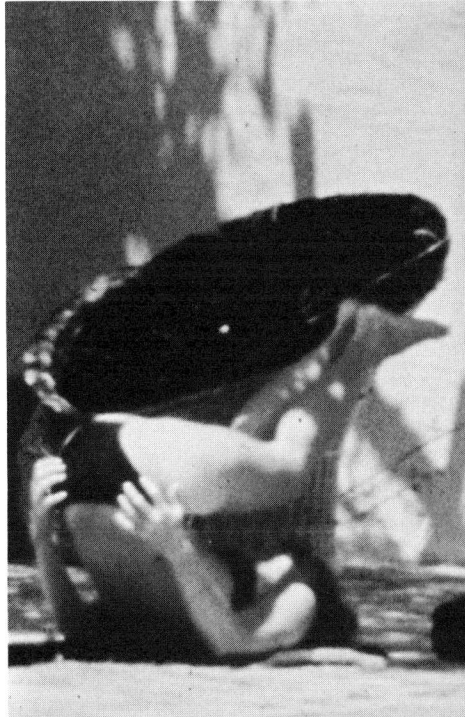

Jackie Onassis demonstrates her skill in offensive yoga which won her a black belt.

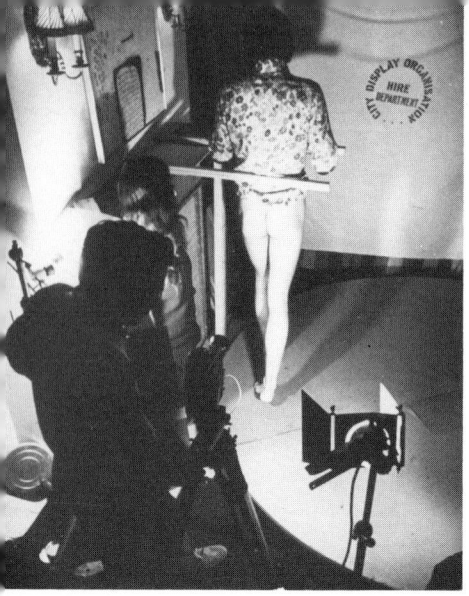

Yoko Ono and friend get down to the bottom line.

The Duchess of York shows her racoon tail.

"Er, it's a family tradition, I suppose," said nubile Sharon Grossout, 19, when asked why she had chosen to embellish her right buttock to celebrate the union of Prince Andrew and Miss Sarah Ferguson. "My mum had the entire cast of EastEnders engraved on her botty," says slinky Sharon, "and that almost counts as royalty, doesn't it?"

owner will necessarily be fat or even approaching plumpness, rather that the buttocks themselves are of formidable proportions relative to the remainder of the person. Many rising orb owners are rightfully proud of their endowment, others find it a problem – usually in terms of clothing it. This is a problem easily solved, however, and well worth the effort it takes to amend your wardrobe. Men with a rising orb profile look magnificent in loose classic-cut trousers, Gatsby trousers and Bermuda shorts (well, *someone* must look good in them!). They should wear their tennis or squash shorts a little longer in length than a man with, say, a hillock profile and should not attempt skin-tight trousers except on rare occasions – such as fancy dress parties when pretending to represent themselves as larger forms of African wildlife. Women with the rising orb profile may particularly suffer from illicit pinches and tweaks both in the place of work and in crowded streets, subways and department stores and everywhere in Italy. The owner should try to take this violation as lightly as possible. Since this profile may stimulate ancient and primal urges (which the perpetrator of the pinch may not themselves recognise), the pincher is entirely hostage to their baser instincts, or so their defence lawyer in court will try to make out. You see, this profile is gently reminiscent of the steatopygous goddesses of our collective past and, as such, it signals deep into the psyche. Clothing the rising orb, if you are a woman, is usually easy if you double-check your purchases in the mirror before laying out the cash and is made easier still if you have rudimentary sewing skills. For instance, hemlines may need to be let down at the rear of skirts and dresses and the waistbands of trousers may need to be taken in (assuming you have had to buy trousers a size larger to fit round your posterior). These precautions apart, you are likely to derive, and supply, considerable enjoyment from your profile.

Famous historical personage exhibiting a rising orb profile: Queen Mary of Scotland, often loyally referred to as 'Queen of Bots'.

2. The Lift Quotient

Now we come to a more technical aspect of the art and science of clunology: the assessment of vertical mobility capability per individual, as well as per pair of, buttocks. This is a simple concept to grasp (wait!) and, as you shall find, an easy manifestation to measure. But first, it is wise to identify the phenomenon in yourself, by feel, and in others, by observation. A thirty-second bout of running on the spot will indicate to you the degree of vertical mobility you enjoy; the same exercise performed by a companion will enable you to observe the phenomenon in another. In this test, observe only the vertical mobility. Do not include other forms of movement – such as swag, wobble or bounce – in your assessment.

You may already suspect what is true: namely, that this assessment may be made only through observation or through hands-on experimentation. This simple choice has made an otherwise dry area of study immensely pleasurable. There is but one rule that demands strict adherence – any second person taking part in these experiments must give their permission, in full awareness of the processes, before any test or measurement is made by hands-on techniques.

Here, then, are the five experiments so essential to understanding vertical mobility capability in the buttock. The student is advised to make a considered assessment of the results of each experiment using a number between one and five. When all five tests are completed, these numbers are totalled to provide the Lift Quotient for that bottom.

The Self-Lift

In this experiment the buttocks are first examined (as a pair) in their standing, relaxed position. Remember, this examination may be performed either through observation or through manual contact. Once the state of relaxation has been established and understood, the owner of the buttocks is asked to lift them by a controlled contraction of their gluteal muscles. In other words, they are to tighten their buttocks so that the cheeks lift in unison.

After holding this position for a minimum of fifteen seconds, the owner may relax the gluteals. However, they should be prepared to repeat the experiment should the student clunologist require more time to make his or her assessment. A popular side-effect of this experiment is an improvement in muscle tone in the owner as well as an increase in circulation and pygal (from the Greek, meaning pertaining to the buttocks) awareness. Many wonderful things have happened as a result. At this point, you should chronicle the assessment made in numerical form.
Score: (out of five)..........................

The Open-Lift

In this experiment both buttocks are gripped firmly at their lower-most edge then lifted firmly and swiftly up and apart. Do not get too carried away here. The movement up and apart is simultaneous and may require a little practice to master. Fortunately, this experiment, though definitely a hands-on technique, may be performed either on one's self or on a willing companion. In both cases, some attention must be paid during practice assessments to perfecting the movement so that it is not unpleasant for the owner of the buttocks. With rare exceptions, however, this experiment has a relaxing and soothing effect and gives pygal awareness a new and extended meaning.

As in the first experiment, the buttocks must be fully relaxed when the assessment begins and, also, they must remain relaxed throughout the experiment. This will be easy when the person performing the assessment practises a gentle and confident movement and the importance of this can, again, not be too strongly stressed. When it can be achieved, the relaxed state of the buttocks throughout the test will enable the student to assess the vertical mobility capability of buttocks when in a semi-open (apart) state.

Again, a number between one and five may be assigned at the outcome of this experiment and chronicled for later use. It is useful to state here that any of these experiments may be repeated as often as wished to achieve the most satisfactory

outcome. Indeed, a great deal of improvement can be expected when the experiments are repeated on a regular basis.
Score: (out of five).........................

The Up-Lift

In this experiment the student should face the willing subject and, reaching round him or her, firmly seize one buttock in each wide-spread hand. Some time may be needed to perfect this starting position. The owner's gluteal muscles should be in a state of complete relaxation, as in the previous experiment, and they should remain relaxed throughout the assessment.

Upon gripping the buttocks in a contented fashion, the student should slowly but definitely lift the buttocks in an unambiguously vertical direction. Both buttocks must move simultaneously. The buttocks should not be pressed inwards so that they clench together and neither should they be pulled 'open' as in the previous experiment. When at the height of their vertical lift, the student should pause to assess the degree of lift. The buttocks must not be dropped having once achieved their maximum lift. Instead, the student's grip on the buttocks must remain confident while he or she lowers the buttocks into their original position. At this point the student may allocate a number between one and five to the results of the experiment; this number should be chronicled.
Score: (out of five).........................

The Squeeze-Lift

In this experiment the buttocks are lifted together, as one unit. The student faces the subject, grips the buttocks firmly in both hands and then *squeezes* the cheeks together. The owner should make every attempt to keep the muscles relaxed throughout this experiment, though a little practice might be necessary to achieve this aim.

Once the buttocks are firmly squeezed in place, the student should lift them as though they were one unit, at all times maintaining the degree of squeeze first accomplished. At the height of this lift, the student should assess the degree of vertical mobility achieved and assign a number between one and five to the result. At this point the buttocks may be lowered into their original position or, and many owners prefer this method, simply released and allowed to drop into place.

The results of this experiment do improve with practice, therefore you may wish to perform it several times before chronicling the numerical results.

Score: (out of five).......................

The Alternate-Lift

This experiment is always conducted last in the Lift series because, by this time the owner should know how to keep his or her buttocks in a state of relaxation and the student should know how to grasp the buttocks with purpose. Both of these conditions are essential to the successful outcome of this experiment.

As in the other experiments of this series, the student faces the subject and firmly grips the buttocks in both hands. In this assessment, however, the student may find it beneficial to bend his or her knees slightly, in order to obtain more leverage. Once the position is corrected the student lifts one buttock in a vertical direction with a definite and slightly rapid thrust of the hand. Upon reaching its apex, the buttock is instantly dropped – though the student's hand should remain in contact with or in close proximity to it.

As the buttock is dropped, the other buttock is lifted in the same manner. This process is repeated several times and a pleasant and controlled rhythm is established. Though perhaps the most skilful of the experiments so far, it also has the greatest potential for pleasure. It is no rare thing for both the student and the subject to be discovered in a state of great hilarity. In addition, the subject often reports a heightened awareness of his or her bottom and the rather sensitive adjacent organs and surrounding area.

Score: (out of five).......................

Finally, you may total the assessment figures derived from this series of experiments to arrive at the Lift quotient:
Lift Quotient: (out of 25).................

3. The Bounce Barometer

This portion of our studies requires that the student leave the security of his or her armchair, front room, padded cell or whatever, in order to do some original field work. No special equipment is required and there is no additional expenditure; in fact, all that is necessary is a keen eye and, perhaps, a small notebook and working pen. Discretion is the keynote. If you get arrested, no one's going to bail you out, and no one's going to believe your story anyway. So if you are unable, for any reason whatsoever, to quietly observe your fellow creatures as they go about their lives, then please stay at home and play with your rattle until you're old enough to be let out alone.

The Unrepentant Clunologist

The purpose of this period in the field is to develop expertise in the observation of bottom bounce and in the accurate assessment of the quality of that bounce. Before we go any further it is best, perhaps, to define and briefly discuss the phenomenon of bounce as applied to bottoms. Bounce is directly related to the vertical mobility capability so well researched in our Lift series of experiments. That is, the bounce is based upon the vertical motion potential within a particular bottom . . . but it is also more than that. A bounce is an unobscured and self-perpetuating movement of the buttocks comprised of an up and down oscillation (of the buttocks) brought on by an outside force or a movement of the whole body.

In the following series of assessments the student must rely entirely on his or her powers of observation. Willing subjects may perform the experiments in a non-threatening environment or the student may simply step out on any day of the week and wait for good fortune to provide the necessary situations, and bottoms, to observe. In each of the experiments that follow, the student is encouraged to observe the movement up and then down again of any buttock or buttocks and to note their numerical assessment (any number between one and five). As a bounce is incomplete unless both an upward and downward movement are involved, the student may wish to spend a considerable length of time in observation of various bottoms before settling on a definitive scale of assessment. Without further ado, then, here are the five experiments which will help the eager student develop an unerring eye for bounce.

The Walking Bounce

It must first be said that a great many bottoms do not bounce when the owner is walking. These are bottoms with little or no surplus fatty tissue, exceptional muscle tone or simply positioned on the body in such a way that they are not jostled by the ambulatory action. However, when you do see a walking bounce, you will find it immediately recognisable.

On each walking step forward, the buttock that bounces will rise a small distance then, while the body weight is shifting to the other leg, the buttock will continue to rise an infinitesimal amount before it drops down into its resting position. Even at this point, depending on the force and speed of the walk, the buttock may display a 'rebound bounce' by again rising slightly after it has dropped. This does not, however, happen in all bouncing bottoms. Should you wish to study the rebound bounce in greater detail, you are advised to regard either a woman in very high heels or a man who places his weight firmly on his heels as he walks.

The full impact of this cluneal collaboration in motion should not be underestimated. Musicians have likened it to a visual interpretation of the timpani section of an orchestral score; poets have scribed its profound relationship with the cosmic pulses of nature. Geronimus L. Grimes, Professor Laureate of Natestistics in the Department of Genetic Engineering and Social Deviation, University of Johannesburg, has declared this bounce 'a barometer of cultural wellbeing' and claims that times and people are happier when the bounce is readily observed. Fully grown (and otherwise stable) men may on occasion sit down and weep after observing an especially ample bounce.

Score: (out of five).........................

The Running Bounce

The act of running naturally increases the percussive force of the foot striking the ground and therefore increases the effect of this force on the motion of the buttocks. A bottom that was noted to bounce when walking will undoubtedly have a more pronounced bounce while running. And bottoms that showed no sign of a walking bounce may, happily, display a definite tendency to bounce when running. So it is important that, given any number of running people, the student extend his or her observation to include all running bottoms.

Many joggers have bouncing bottoms. Crowded city streets during the rush hours are also prolific with running people and the occasional running bounce may be spotted. Many people do not like the sensation of owning a running bounce and will cease running immediately they feel it. This not only causes

many people to miss trains and buses, it also deprives the student clunologist of research material. Therefore, it is hoped that this book will, to some degree, influence the shy and self-conscious into relaxing and letting their bounces happen.
Score: (out of five)........................

The Slow-Dance Bounce

Some people are endowed with bottoms that bounce at any encouragement – think, for instance, of those bounces which may be observed while sitting overlooking a dance floor. Admittedly, one should consider it a rare and fortunate experience when it happens, yet it is possible to spot bottoms that bounce with no further encouragement than a sweet and simple slow dance.

This bounce is caused, in part, by the sometimes awkward position of the owner's body (some dancers arch and slouch in the most peculiar ways) which exaggerates the rise and fall of the bouncing buttock. However, it would not occur at all had not the owner a particularly mobile natal (from the Latin *nates* for buttocks) region. On no account should you mistake a wobble for a bounce. Avoid this error if you wish to maintain a clear comprehension of all that the bottom is capable. The bounce is a vertical movement, whereas the wobble (see next series) is a side to side movement.
Score: (out of five)........................

The Sudden-Move Bounce

In common with the earthquake (which it resembles), it is impossible to predict the frequency with which this bounce may be observed. In fact, its occurrence at all is entirely dependent upon luck and even more luck is required for it to be spotted. The experienced student of clunology might develop a 'sixth sense' regarding this bounce and may often find him or herself lifting their gaze just in time to see the bouncing outcome of a sudden movement. Any sudden movement can cause this bounce. It has been spotted in short men who move quickly from sitting to standing position; in women who are startled

by the movement of a lift, in people who have just realised that someone else is about to reach for the restaurant bill. You may even observe this phenomenon on buses when, as the bus brakes unexpectedly, the standing occupants are forced to fight for their balance. Spotting this bounce requires the intervention of good fortune and the student should prepare him or herself to assess the bounce quickly and accurately when luck presents it to them. It can, however, be one of the most sastisfying of all bounces to observe, being 'a veritable rictus on the Richter scale', according to Professor Grimes.
Score: (out of five)......................

The Climbing Bounce

This bounce may be spotted on any working day by simply observing men and women walking or running up the stairs at their places of work. The exaggerated movement of their legs (when compared to flat-terrain walking) and the jarring effect of hard shoes on hard steps increases the likelihood of a bounce occurring. Though not always equalling the size of a running bounce, this bounce is extremely satisfying to observe and assess – if only because it goes on for between seven and thirteen steps, on average. In addition, it is generally a graceful and rhythmic bounce which further enhances its appeal. The hidden danger in this type of bounce, if it is continued over any long period of time, lies in the fact that a standing waveform may be generated which, with its increasing amplitude, could seriously damage items of clothing, nearby masonry and spectators. Just such an event occurred in the so-called 'Great Rump Disaster' of 1945 in Durban, where several hundred people suffered severe contusions while foolishly attempting to set a new world record for non-stop jitterbugging. Professor Grimes theorises, perhaps somewhat romantically, that the Great Pyramids may have been constructed by a civilisation able to harness this mighty force of nature for constructive purposes.
Score: (out of five)......................

4. The Wobble/Weight Index

In this series of tests, the buttocks are assessed for their ability to move freely in all directions, including up and down, diagonally and from side to side, while in a state of relaxed musculature. Although these tests may be performed upon oneself, they are best administered to a close friend or willing subject in order to achieve a clear idea of the movement potential of a given bottom. As usual, the student is advised to make a record of his or her assessment using a number between one and five.

The wobble was once described as a 'tantalising shimmer of movement emanating freely from the conjugation of flesh and interruptive motion' by Geronimus L. Grimes. His assertion that the cluneal wobble was crucial to the development of numerical skills, contrapuntal musical composition and political deviance has certainly endured much criticism over the years. The authors of the present work have, in fact, been among those to have strongly questioned his conclusions and, indeed, his motives. Nevertheless, Professor Grimes's highly controversial theory cannot be lightly dismissed – as he is quick to point out, no other hypothesis comes close to explaining the sheer number of South African politicians whose names all begin with 'BOT'.

By adding a crucial factor to Grimes's judgement of the beauty and cultural significance of the cluneal wobble, one may establish a fail-safe method of correctly assessing the quality of wobble in any given bottom. This element is weight, specifically: the weight of each buttock. This factor is set against the degree of wobble perceived, and the two are calculated to arrive at one figure: the Wobble/Weight Index. Studies are currently in progress (Professor Grimes has kindly offered his services, and South African regulations regarding the ethics of important sociological experiments such as these are extremely accommodating) which will interpret the relationship between the average Index in a population and socio-cultural development together with political deviance. As these are epidemiological studies (i.e. they involve infecting large numbers of people with epidemics), it may be some years before the results and conclusions are available.

Students will have ample opportunity to develop an 'eye' for the assessment of wobble so that, eventually, they may calculate the index of a bottom just by looking. However, to start with it is important to have hands-on experience as this will ensure an accurate and unbiased assessment. In each of the following tests, the student faces the subject (who should be standing), reaches round the subject and firmly cradles one buttock in the palm of each hand. The subject should ensure that the buttock muscles remain relaxed throughout the experiments.

The Weighty Lift & Lower

In this experiment, the student slowly lifts the buttocks until he or she senses the weight of each buttock. Although this may be performed one buttock at a time, more expertise is developed if the student performs the double-buttock version straight away. Having sensed the weight of each buttock, the student slowly lowers them back into their resting position. This half of the experiment should be repeated as often as necessary, until the student has an accurate sense of cluneal weight.

The very same lift and lower exercise is performed again, but now the student should actually look at the subject's buttocks and make careful note of any changes in shape or appearance. If fully clothed, the buttocks will only reveal a change of shape. If fully unclothed, however, the student may discover dimples, creases and other interesting features that were previously overlooked. Observation of these features will help the student to recognise the signs of weight-induced movement in the buttocks, thus greatly speeding his or her calculation of the wobble/weight index in a variety of situations.

Score: (out of five)......................

The Lift, Drop & Watch Test

Using the same starting position as that indicated above, the student should grip the relaxed buttocks and gently but unambiguously lift them to their maximum height. Some attention may be given to assessing the weight of the subject's buttocks during this time, especially if the student is unfamiliar with them. Upon reaching their apex, the student should release his or her hold on the buttocks and allow them to drop forcefully into their resting position.

When this exercise is successfully accomplished, the student must alter his or her position so that they may observe the buttocks as they drop. A seated position will afford maximum comfort and uninterrupted view. Any student worried about the occupational hazards involved in sitting in such a crooked position should bear in mind that the position is held for a very brief time and no physical damage could possibly result.

The full experiment may be repeated several times in order that the student has ample opportunity to observe how the dropping weight of the buttock causes a distinct wobble in the buttock or, indeed, the whole bottom. If these tests are done in sequence, this may be the first time the student has observed the wobble phenomenon at such close range and he or she should be forgiven for wishing to repeat the experiment an inordinate number of times.

Score: (out of five).........................

The Lift with Vertical Wobble

Having observed, in no uncertain terms, the first indications of wobble in a buttock, it remains for the student to explore the full potential of this movement. In order to keep a clear and uncompromising grip on the concept of wobble, this test and the two that follow will explore specific types of wobble. However, as in many scientific studies, dissecting a concept into its finer parts does not make for a whole concept. The student must always bear in mind that the wobble is complete in itself and that studies made of part-wobbles or aspects-of-wobbles are only in an attempt to heighten the student's understanding of the whole wobble.

In this experiment, therefore, the student should first and foremost open his or her senses to what might follow. Assuming the typical starting position for this series of tests, the student should grip one buttock in the palm of each hand then lift the subject's buttocks in a directly vertical manner until they have reached their apex.

The student should now peer around the subject so that the buttocks may be easily observed. At this point, and retaining a firm grip, the buttocks should be given a brisk up-and-down shake involving approximately four movements of the fingers. If the subject's gluteals become tense, the student should reposition his or her fingers in order to encourage complete muscular relaxation in the subject. Repeat this experiment as often as is necessary to achieve a vertical wobble of the cluneal flesh. Close observation of the phenomenon may assist the student in correct placement of his or her fingers as well as the appropriate degree of wobble to promote.

Score: (out of five)......................

The Lift with Horizontal Wobble

Perhaps the most memorable wobble of all, the horizontal variety enjoys the distinction of being quite unlike the vertical movements involved in either Lift or Bounce. It is a side-to-side tremor of flesh that lasts only a portion of a second, leaving but a fleeting impression of soft promise in the eye of the beholder.

To fully capture the essence of the horizontal wobble, the student should proceed as in the previous experiments, settling into a comfortable position from which to both grip and view. Immediately both the student and the subject are ready, the buttocks should be lifted to approximately half their height potential. Held in this position, the student may squeeze them playfully between his or her thumb and forefinger to ascertain their degree of relaxation. If the gluteals are tense, the subject should be urged to relax them.

When, at last, the buttocks are held in the semi-elevated position the student should shake them quickly and briskly from side to side to cause a horizontal wobble. The student should be certain to observe the whole of this experiment in order to benefit from all it has to offer. An assessment may be made only after the student has become proficient at the mechanics of this performance.

Once expertise is gained, the student may wish to provoke a horizontal wobble by the simple and ancient means of prodding one or both buttocks with the forefinger. In a sufficiently fleshy subject, this action will result in a delightful wobble, though less lengthy than that just described.

Score: (out of five)........................

The Whole Bottom Wobble

Before exploring the final test in the wobble series, the student may wish to compare the degree of wobble possible from one buttock to the other. There are no hard and fast procedures to follow here as this is a way of learning which is personal to the student and should therefore be personally designed. Suffice it to say that a playful approach to the comparison of one buttock to its partner is a most satisfactory attitude to harbour.

Having had one's temporary fill of such comparative analysis, the student should desert his or her position of facing the subject and, instead, stand or sit facing the subject's buttocks. The student should open his or her hands and place them flat, one against the outer side of each buttock. Ensure at this point that the subject's buttocks are in a state of complete relaxation and that the subject is standing comfortably.

With a slow build-up of speed, the student should tenderly pat one buttock then the other with a sideways movement of the hand against the cheek. The result is a most emphatic wobble of both cheeks accompanied by a rather comforting slapping sound. The student should avoid too much enthusiasm in his or her patting movement, lest the experiment turn into a study of spanking. Instead, the motive must remain the observation of wobble when induced in the whole bottom.

This accomplished, the student may maintain the experiment for several minutes, or as long as the subject is contented. Assessment of the wobble may be made solely on degree and quality of the wobble or, at the student's discretion, may

include the visual bonuses of dimpling, creasing and slight reddening of the skin.
Score: (out of five).........................
Total score: (out of twenty-five)...................

5. The Cleavage Classification

In recent times the subject of an oppressive and irrational taboo, the cluneal cleavage is currently reclaiming its popularity. It is written in many of the ancient Central Thracian manuscripts (which culture worshipped the physique) that mystical women (known as *pairospexes*) could tell one's fortune by a brief probing of the cluneal cleavage. Indeed, many happy marriages were contracted on the strength of this belief in cluneal forecasting. Sadly, that art has been lost to the past, but recent research (see '*Pygmies, pygalia and capital*

The Pairospex Probing the Cluneal Cleavage

punishment', Grimes, G. L., Thumbscrew Press, Bloemfontein, 1955) has established five broad categories of cleavage, into which most people's divides may be classified. The following are distinct categories which preclude further numerical assessment. The student should become acquainted with the distinctions described and then do his or her best to allocate a specific bottom to one of these categories. Of course, some cleavages will bear the characteristics of more than one category and the student must feel free to recognise and analyse such composite forms. Cleavage recognition is a skill which one may develop over many years and which will ripen into a most impressive and unerring talent, entertaining at parties and helpful in providing light relief during those difficult moments at funerals.

The Rainforest Cleavage

A distinctive cleavage indeed — populated by a dense tangle of often matted hair which climbs some distance up the subject's back and, in extreme cases, joins with the hairline at the neck. Usually seen in builders, plasterers, brick layers, commodities traders, double glazing salespeople and pop stars proclaiming their concern for South American coca forests, acid-house rain, greenhouses, etc. This cleavage may be observed on any urban street where there are obvious signs of building work in progress. It is often accompanied by an over-fed and over-hanging gut which hangs disconsolately to the floor. The Rainforest is by no means pleasing from the front, but is much worse from the rear, for there, in full view, is a sweaty, podgy, cleavage with plaster-caked hairs (N.B. in commodities traders, pop stars etc. the substance may actually be *Homme Cher* talcum powder, but the effect is more or less indistinguishable). Not something you really want to take a second look at, much less make a study of. Before you are able to turn, gagging, in the other direction, however, the man invariably bends or crouches so that his trousers are pulled down still further at the back. You are forced to watch, transfixed, while a rivulet of perspiration trickles down the tunnel of his protruding posterior into the darkness of his awful trousers. Three words will summarise the experience and the phenomenon: repulsive, repulsive, repulsive.

The Convergent Cleavage

Like two ski-slopes plunging towards conclusion, this cleavage sports a daring curve which is at once concise and mildly overstated. 'This cleavage begs, nay beseeches, one to touch it' states Geronimus L. Grimes in his seminal work entitled *My Seminal Work*, 'and to trace its irresistible lines from the meeting place of back with buttocks, downwards and inwards as the edges of the buttocks bulge closer and closer and closer . . . then converge in soft intimacy an inch or two further along, like a Table Mountain of the soul.'

This cleavage should be lightly greased from time to time with a suitable oil (nothing intended for industrial or mechanical use, although an edible oil such as soya or sunflower would be most appropriate and very good for your companion's cholesterol level). The skin will remain soft, velvety and uncreased if this practice is continued on a daily basis.

The Death Valley Cleavage

Very thin people and those with broad hips (whether male or female) are among the most likely to have this distinctive cleavage. The characteristics are unmistakable: the buttocks curve inward from their tops and slope gracefully and poetically down until they swell into completion and resolve into the thighs. Never once do the inner edges of the two buttocks meet, so that this cleavage is, in some senses, no cleavage at all.

However, provided the owner is not *too* thin, this cleavage remains one of the most sought after in the world. Says Professor Grimes: 'It is a veritable celebration of "the apartheid of the posterior", emphasising, as it does, the independence and uniqueness of each buttock within each pair.' The student who is given access to a Death Valley will note, also, that the entire coccygeal region is presented in a clear and prominent manner as a result of this cleavage. Thus, an excellent opportunity is created for the student to become acquainted with further aspects of the bony structure upon which the bottom is positioned.

The Long, Thin Line Cleavage

With barely a hint of curve at the top of each cheek, the buttocks rush together in a collision of flesh to form a long, thin line. This cleavage is strangely seductive, especially when partially clothed in a swimsuit or pair of silky knickers. For there is a sense of infinity in this line and the student may feel something stirring deep within his or her soul upon observing this cleavage for the first time. The insistent relocation of the cheeks into their impressive crease after the buttocks have been gently prised apart is a phenomenon much written and talked of in learned South African circles. The student should make every attempt to read these remarks in anticipation of discovering a long, thin line cleavage in the course of their studies.

The Touch and Go Cleavage

A startling manifestation of symmetry, and perhaps the most fascinating and rare form of cleavage. The essential feature of the Touch and Go cleavage is that the curve from the top of the buttock to the meeting of cheeks is *identical* to the curve from the bottom of the buttock to the meeting of cheeks! Thus the cleavage is but a brief and tentative meeting point of flesh that is precisely centred in the map of this posterior. However the space is dissected, still the cleavage is central and all curves related to its occurrence are symmetrical.

6. The Rear View

A powerful remnant of our evolutionary past, the human preoccupation with observing the rear has never waned, particularly the instinct to focus a voracious gaze directly onto a full-posterior display. No profile, no hands-on experimentation, just a straightforward, all-embracing look at the cluneal characteristics directly *en face* or, perhaps, *en fesse*. To illustrate the magic of the Rear View, one can do little better than quote the introductory lines from the terminal thesis of Spiro van den Smuts, one of Professor Grimes' most gifted protégés, intriguingly entitled '*Natal: Latin for Buttocks or South Africa's Smallest State?*': 'The Rear View creates perhaps, more anticipation and lust than any other form of bottom evaluation. The surprises are greater, the rewards more satisfying, the disappointments less important when the View is eventually transposed into contact and active assessment. For the Rear View is, in some respects, a painting, a two-dimensional description which rouses the inner passions but never communes with them. Quite simply, once touched and explored from other perspectives, the Rear View ceases to exist. Therefore it is forever there, in the distance, yet mercifully inaccessible.'

The quasi-spiritual terms in which all discussions of the Rear View are couched may, at first, alarm the earnest student. Yet, undoubtedly, they too will find that it is the only means of dealing with the Rear View phenomenon in the verbal medium. Further, the student should be aware at the outset that the assessment of Rear View will never – can never – be conclusive! For, as Smuts points out, 'it is impossible to reconcile the facts of contact and measurement with the perception and ideology of viewing'.

Here then are a handful of commonly observed Rear Views with which the student should become acquainted. All observations should be made at a minimum distance of approximately eight feet (metric equivalent 2.5 metres) to prevent an inadvertent and simultaneous assessment of profile, curve and so on. While these descriptions mark five distinct forms, some blurring of the boundaries does occur and the student may well encounter a bottom that happily merges 'Peach' type with, for instance, 'Pear' type. The resulting fruit salad is likely to be most alluring.

Peaches

Consider two peaches, complete with fine downy velvet, firmly affixed to two aspiring thighs and you will begin to understand the vision of a Peaches Rear View. As the name and imagery denote, this View is an uncompromising Shakespearian world view of the buttocks as two globes. A nearly definite circumference of flesh rounds proudly up, to the sides, down and inward to claim spherical prominence.

Pears

Here, again as the name implies, two pears hang precariously from the thin and fragile stem of spine. The buttocks wait and wait before they burst into fruition at their lower edges. This vision is alluring to those who dream of fecund females and/or tender, underworked young men. There is usually an accompaniment of pout to this view which is obvious by the dark fold line at the underside of each cheek.

Bunches of Grapes

The Bunches of Grapes Rear View involves a paradigm-shift in perception which, for many people, is a wholly distasteful experience. This type of bottom has been out of fashion for several generations. As a result, there is only the merest recollection of its particular quality of beauty in the collective memory and the student, consequently, may find it difficult to endure. Nevertheless, one must summarise this View so that the student may accurately and without hesitation recognise and observe it. The Bunches of Grapes is essentially a lumpy vision with clusters of flesh emerging at sudden, unusual and rather frightening angles and positions on the rear anatomy. To say it is a dimpled view would be to grossly understate the experience, the more so if the view is of a naked bottom. Upon movement, this bottom combines the phenomena of bounce, wobble and sway more surprisingly and with more profound effect than any other bottom. So it is that many students, though initially inclined to disgorge their lunches at the sight of this rear, may well experience a state of near-mesmerisation some two or three minutes later. Simply, the Bunches of Grapes is cacophony in motion and one feels awesome respect for it despite one's personal preferences. (Historical note: many of the bottoms which appear in paintings by Peter Paul Rubens were originally 'bunches of grapes' genotypes with some fairly expensive studio retouching and airbrush work added to make the result more pleasing and less libelous).

Acorns

As any oak tree knows, acorns have a considerable potential for growth and so, with this in mind, the Acorn Rear View is named. But the similarity continues when one compares the shape of this bottom with that of an acorn still encased in its shell. The extended width of the acorn's casing, set beneath a slim and acceptable nut are clearly like the extended width of an upper thigh set beneath a slim and acceptable buttock. The lines are unmistakable and, for the owner of the bottom, the dangers are clear: if this bottom is not well cared for, the cluneal version of a mighty oak will surely grow.

The Acorn is a largely female possession which is clearly visible whether clothed or unclothed; therefore the student may find this an easy Rear View to recognise. Should the student become acquainted with the owner, a quiet word about muscle tone and daily exercise would not go amiss. Yet, we should not imply disfavour as regards the Acorn – if well cared for it can offer a visual summary of lithe beauty.

Peanuts

Some bottoms simply disappear off the face of the pygal map when viewed from the rear and this View is one of them. Here the buttocks are so demure and lacking in fleshy substance that they appear nonexistent. Owners tend to be in estate agency, public relations, hairdressing or debt collecting, their eyes are usually set too close together, their eyebrows often join in the middle of the forehead, and they are, in summary, by no means trustworthy. No shadows, lines, creases or insinuations of bulk are visible from the point of observation and the student may feel so astounded by this fact that he or she may move forward to perform a hands-on experiment before realising what they are doing. Watch it, or faster than you can say 'jacksy-pardy' you'll either end up in court or flat on your back in an Armenian deathlock.

Peanuts are quite a rare vision in the nude, yet that is the only way to make an accurate assessment of them. Clothed, especially in loose skirt or trousers, the suspected Peanut may hide features which lift it out of this category. It is best to be certain and the student should either request an unclothed viewing or, preferably, walk quickly away.

7. Tone Testing

The gluteal muscles are the foundation for the modern bottom. As discussed in chapter one, immediately humans became bipedal and began to walk and run in an upright position, the exact position and function of these muscles altered. Thus the human bottom lifted and became more prominent than those of our fellow primates. Add to this the increased layer of pygal fat and one can quickly see how the human posterior has remained legendary for so long a time.

The late twentieth century bottom is no different from those first humanoid bottoms – except, perhaps, that fewer of us walk and run. And the result of this omission is that fewer of us have well developed gluteals, leading to loose and floppy bottoms, back ache, poorly positioned fatty tissue and excess wobble, bounce and sway.

In this series of experiments, the student is encouraged to test for the tone of the gluteal muscles using one or more of five well researched methods. After each test, please assess the outcome using a number between one and five.

The Prod and Poke Method

Both the subject and the student should stand for this test, the subject in front of the student. Whether clothed or unclothed, the subject should maintain complete relaxation of the gluteal muscles while the student presses one or more fingers simultaneously into each buttock. The student may prod from the side or the rear, as is their preference, and make note of the depth to which their fingers are able to poke. This movement is an unhurried movement which the student may repeat several times, if necessary. What is the sensation? Is it cold porridge, dry sand, pizza dough, or squashed entrails?

At the student's request, the subject should tense his or her gluteal muscles and hold them tensed while the student repeats the prodding movement. This time, however, the student's fingers are unlikely to submerge so deeply into the fleshy orbs and the student must note the difference in depth between the relaxed and tensed muscle prod. An assessment should be made before moving on to the next test.

Score: (out of five).........................

The Handful Method

Probably the most agreeable method of testing the degree of gluteal muscle tone. Both the student and the subject stand, the subject in front with his or her gluteals completely relaxed. The student then cups one buttock in one hand and slowly but firmly grips the relaxed flesh. This grip should be maintained while the student notes the approximate size of the pygal handful they are holding. The grip is then released. If desired, the other buttock may be tested in the same way.

The test is repeated but, instead of releasing the grip, the subject is asked to tense his or her gluteal muscles as much as possible and to maintain this tension. As the gluteals tense, the student observes how the size of their handful diminishes, if at all, and to what degree. Some people with exceptional muscle tone are able to free their buttock completely from the student's grip; others have poor muscle tone and are scarcely able to reduce the size of the student's handful at all. In all

cases the student must use any alteration in size of handful to assess the tone of the subject's gluteal muscles. A number between one and five should be selected as a means of chronicling this assessment.
Score: (out of five).......................

The Twopenny Piece Method

Although long a feature of vaudeville acts and young farmers' parties, this test does, in fact, provide an accurate means of assessing the tone of gluteal muscles, particularly in terms of their potential for sustained tension. This test is quick and easy to perform, though it does require a special effort on the part of the subject.

The student first takes a twopenny piece and warms it to blood temperature by running it under warm water. The subject then stands and presents his or her cluneal cleavage to the student, who holds the warmed coin about mid-point in the subject's cleavage. At the student's request, the subject tenses his or her gluteal muscles in an attempt to grip the coin with sufficient force to enable the student to let go of it. The student should note the success of this attempt and assign a number between one and five to the results.

Some people – those with Death Valley cleavages, for instance – are biologically unable to grip the coin at all, therefore this test may be amended to suit their anatomy. In the amended version, the subject tightens his or her muscles and keeps them tightened while the student attempts, albeit gently, to prize them further apart with a simple 'reverse pinching' movement of the thumb and forefinger inserted mid-point in the cleavage. The degree of opposition the student feels will help him or her to accurately assess the tone of the gluteal muscles.
Score: (out of five).......................

The Seated Leap Method

This is the power-gesture in the body language of the bottom. One can occasionally see both elderly male chimpanzees in the wild and executive passengers travelling first-class on Concorde performing this activity in absent-minded contentment. It is a natural movement which is a powerful indicator of, as well as improver of, gluteal strength and tone. Both the student and the subject will find it a simple and rewarding examination of the innate power within the bottom. In his book *The Decline of the West*, Oswald Spengler makes the point that the Nazi salute undoubtedly has its roots in this tightening of the buttocks, starting first as a spasm of the cheeks inwards, spreading up the stiffening spinal column, and culminating as a sudden and violent erection of the right arm. To which Professor Grimes adds that the biological inability of certain racial groups (socialists, ecologists, vegetarians, etc) to perform this simple action is clear evidence of their genetic inferiority.

The subject should sit upright on a firm-seated stool or chair with his or her feet flat on the floor in front of them. The student, meanwhile, should procure a measuring stick of at least one metre in length and place it upright behind and just touching the subject's spine. The student should note what point on the measure marks the top of the subject's head. At the student's request the subject should tighten both buttocks as much as possible so that his or her body rises a little. a few quick practice attempts can be made, then the tensed buttock position should be held for at least five seconds while the student notes the new point on the measuring stick which marks the top of the subject's head.

When satisfied that an accurate reading has been obtained, the student should compare the difference in height achieved between the relaxed buttock position and the tightened buttock position. This difference may be as little as 1cm but with the possibility of totalling several centimetres. The student may summarise his or her assessment by considering this figure as well as the length of time the lift was held and the control the subject maintained while in the tight-buttocked position. A number between one and five will be an adequate summary.
Score: (out of five).......................

The Rhythm Method

This is a delightful means of assessing the tone of gluteal muscles which will appeal to Catholics, Protestants and all others of distinct religious persuasions – in fact, both the student and the subject seem to derive a great deal of pleasure and amusement from performing this test. The student is an observer in this method and does not require any props, rulers or riding crops. The subject is in control and may display whatever rhythmic talents he or she has when performing the rhythmic release.

The student should make him or herself comfortable in a seated position some distance behind the standing subject. At the student's request, the subject should contract and release the gluteal muscles in first one buttock, then the other. This rhythmic movement may be fast or slow, at the subject's discretion, but should never become indistinct. In other words, the contraction and the release of the contraction should be as definite and complete as possible. Only if this is ensured can the student make an accurate assessment of gluteal tone. Before he disappeared under extremely suspicious circumstances, the young Spiro van den Smuts apparently spent several weeks each year touring the theatres and clubs of Rhodesia and Southern Africa with an absolutely riveting performance based upon his personal mastery of the Rhythm Method, set to a medley of themes from Strauss waltzes and Wagnerian operas. One cannot but feel that the world is the poorer for his much lamented disappearance.

Score: (out of five)......................
Total score: (out of twenty-five)..................

8. The Sway Factor

Few things in life are more pleasurable than watching the bottom of a moving person. One can learn so much just from the way the bottom is carried, in particular the degree of pygal awareness the bottom's owner possesses. This part of our studies deals with the phenomenon of sway, that is: the side to side movement of the bottom when observed either as a distinct unit or as part of the whole moving body.

There are many forms of sway, but the five major categories are discussed below. Combinations and permutations of these categories are common and the student is advised to make creative assessments which account for these possibilities. Further, cluneal sway is often manipulated by its owner in order to achieve a specific effect or to communicate a non-verbal message. The student should open him or herself to these communications in order to broaden understanding of the natal vocabulary.

The Single Buttock Sway

This is an unusual phenomenon which is considered so attractive that it is often unsuccessfully mimicked by the more fashionable of stage and television artists. In its authentic form the owner achieves a crisp side to side movement of one buttock, then the other, while walking at a leisurely pace. Each buttock completes its sideways movement, and subsequent return to starting position, within the length of time it takes to make the next step. No amount of training of willing students has, so far, enabled the College of Clunology to reproduce this sway. It seems, quite simply, to be an original, inherited trait. There is only one form of mimickry and it is accomplished by a small shuffling movement, backward and forward, to take the place of a real walk, along with an alternating slight bend of first one knee then the other. Unless executed very deftly, the owner may look as though he or she is desperate to urinate. Professor Grimes recounts (*Honky Haunches: The Gestation of a Social Phenomenon*, Tourniquet Press, 1984) that the emergence of the Afro-American community in the 1960s and '70s as a significant and volatile force within America, combined with the hurried efforts of the white community to show acceptance, evolved a collection of new words, new fashions, new music and new body movements. The single buttock sway, in its authentic form, was more common to (but not exclusive to) the Afro-American population at that time and it seems likely that the imitation of this sway was first attempted during this period. Certainly there are no records of the imitative form appearing before this time, nor in any other country. The authentic version, on the other hand, has a long history of appearing in a selected few of most races and cultures on earth.

The Collision Sway

This sway is most common in women of formidable size who own especially prominent buttocks. The significant feature of this sway is the seeming independence of each buttock: as the owner walks, one buttock begins to swing freely out and to the side. The other follows in the same direction a split-second later – just as the first buttock is returning on an inward-bound sway. The result is a collision which creates a distinct wobble in both buttocks, but also perpetuates the same pattern of movement of both buttocks in the opposite direction.

Watching a person with this sway is a time-consuming pastime; one wonders with amazement why the owner is not carried well off balance from the sheer force and velocity of the sway. Like the previous sway, the Collision Sway is not a very common sight, therefore the student should treat any opportunity to observe one of these as of the utmost importance to his or her studies.

The Rolling Sway

Often denotes a fully developed, sexually at ease and emotionally mature person, and certainly the most anatomically correct way of moving one's bottom. The Rolling Sway combines a semi-rotational movement of the pelvis with a relaxed, though fully functional, use of the buttock muscles. Men and women alike are owners of this sway and in neither sexes does it seem out of place. While it can be learned, it nevertheless appears as a totally natural and health-giving style of moving – which it is. People who know how to walk (i.e. for miles and miles and for days and days) are almost certain to possess this sway. That is because the body naturally selects this as the best way of using the muscles and joints of the pelvic region.

The first step in learning to recognise this sway is to try and perform it yourself. Then, to augment your understanding, you should perform the next two forms of sway and compare them to this one. Having acquired an 'inner' understanding of the movement, you are more likely to recognise it when you see it.

The Pivot Sway

Ask a companion to stand in front of you in a relaxed fashion. Now grip their pelvis from behind and ask them to begin a slow walk around the room – with you bringing up the rear end. As they walk, push one side of their pelvis, then the other, forward and back again so that the pelvis seems to pivot backwards and forwards on the end of their spine.

Your companion may not find this the most comfortable movement, and in any case, it's one that should be avoided. Once you have understood the mechanics of this sway, try performing it yourself. Finally, see if you can spot a Pivot Sway in a perfect stranger and observe the other physical quirks and characteristics which accompany it.

The Lumbar Sway

Just as the Rolling Sway indicates a mature personality, this sway indicates an immature personality which is lacking in confidence. There is a sense that the person is trying far too hard and achieving far too little in the way of sways when the Lumbar Sway is observed. The students will find this an easy sway to perform for themselves and therefore a fairly easy one to recognise.

The use of 'lumbar' in this description confines the motive for this sway to the lumbar region of the spine – also called the 'small of the back' or the 'lower back'. So, instead of the sway evolving from the buttocks themselves or from the natural rotation of the pelvis, this sway is caused by the owner forcefully pushing the whole pelvis (the hips) to one side then the other. The result is a contrived cat-walk movement which one would expect from little girls pretending to have Marilyn Monroe-type hips. It combines ugliness, derision and clumsiness into one long and ghastly gesture.

Moreover, this movement is not confined to women – many men use it too, especially if they feel they have no hips to speak of. Here, some blame must be placed on the vagaries of fashion; some of the very baggy trouser designs, for instance, do not allow a hipless man to appear enticing *unless* a very exaggerated walking movement is practised. Nevertheless, both the student and any lay readers are earnestly requested to discourage the Lumbar Sway in those they know. It can cause problems with the lower spine and the hip joints in later life and can mislead an innocent observer into thinking the Swayer is pretentious beyond toleration.

9. The Curve Component

Having considered the phenomenon of Sway, you will realise that the bottom cannot exist for long without involving other parts of the anatomy. 'The springbok does not leap with its buttocks alone', says Professor Grimes. In this series of tests, the student is taught to observe and calculate the significance of Curve – in and around the bottom – as a determinant of beauty. There are no hard and fast rules which can be applied to the concept of curve; after all, this is not a mathematics textbook. However, there are generations of observation and opinion which bequeath us, by a sort of consensus, a set of guidelines for assessment of this most pleasing of lines. This aspect of clunology must be a long-term study: there are no short-cuts by which one may acquire the true sensitivity gained only by years of critical observation and poetic contemplation of the essence of the curve.

The Stomach Curve

In this era of fashionably flat or hollow stomachs, the owner of a soft or protruding stomach may feel somewhat gecko-like, or even unattractive. This attitude must be extricated from the sufferer's mind. The curve of a stomach can do more to make a bottom, especially in profile, seem attractive to an onlooker than almost any of the curves described here. Exactly how attractive depends upon the size of the duodenal curve.

The student is far enough into these studies to realise that art is present in most aspects of clunology and, presuming upon this realisation, we may now state that, often, the outward curve of a stomach is precisely what is needed to create balance in the overall line and substance of a body. This is especially so when the subject is endowed with a fairly prominent posterior. A huge bottom adjacent to a hollow stomach does little to please the eye and promises even less to the imagination. However, add a soft curve to the line of stomach and the subject instantly becomes more alluring, more graceful in profile, more realistic. Women are fortunate in that they are somehow expected to have a soft, curvacious stomach. Men, on the other hand, soon fail to appeal once greed and sloth inexorably combine to force their stomachs to curve outward and hence exceed the curvature of their bottoms.

Students may look to study the art of the Old Masters in order to augment their comprehension of the stomach/bottom relationship as many of these paintings depict men and women of ample proportions and uninhibited curvaceousness.

The Thigh Curve

The thighs are the two pedestals which contrive to support the bottom, but they also serve to help define the bottom. A flabby, scrawny, lumpish, oafen, flaccid, pendulous, scraggling thigh will do little to entice the eye upwards, toward the bottom. And should the eye stray in that direction, it is likely that what it sees will constitute an unmemorable observation, full of disappointment and arrested intention. But catch sight of a confident, curving thigh and the eye eagerly aspires to the remainder of the vision.

The curve of thigh enhances the characteristics of the bottom so that it becomes more definite, more defined, itself. A long thigh with a distinct forward curve will make you expect a firm and pouting bottom; a stout, ever-thickening thigh will delight you by resolving into a sturdy and slightly dimpled rear. Both are somehow just what your trained eye expected.

There are, as in most things, exceptions to such happy resolutions, however. No one, whether student or lay person, can resist a long, hard stare at the occasional combination of skinny, square thighs with a vast and tear-dropped bottom, for instance. And equally, fascinatingly repulsive are the minute bottoms of hard-core muscle-men combined, inevitably, with their grotesquely hugh thighs, bulging and curving every which way. But this is a freak-show – as a student you must learn to observe whatever appears, of course, but you must also remember you are in a position, as a professional, to give advice and initiate reforms that will elevate the importance placed on the curve of thigh as related to the bottom.

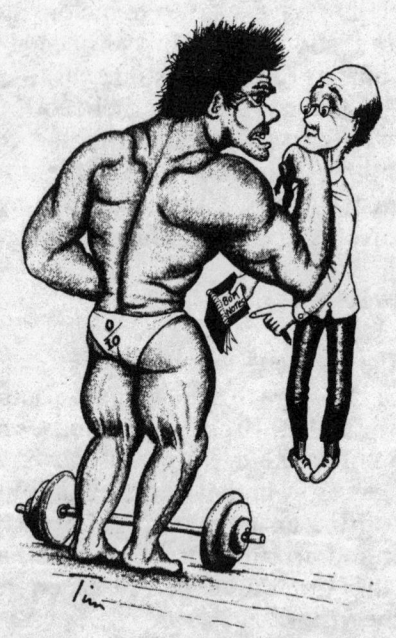

The Professional Clunologist Giving Advice

The Size of Curve

In concise terms, the size of a curve must create balance between the remaining lines and curves. If it does not, then one should attempt to alter the size of one or more curves. For example: a man with a hugh beer-gut and a nearly non-existent bottom has a gross imbalance in his profile. The student of clunology should carefully observe the contrasts of curve within any one body, particularly relating to the bottom, to acquire a sensitive eye for this element of attraction.

The Broken Curve

The most common cause of a broken curve is the interference of elastic-legged knickers, or other restraining garments, which cut into the curving flesh and forever confound its completion. Certainly these are among the most devastating inventions and can have dire consequences for those who over-react to unfulfilled promises. Far better for men and women alike to go without drawers altogether or, if they are considered essential, to select and wear those that most emphatically do not break the pygal curve at precisely the point when it is gaining in impact.

Other broken curves include the disappearance of a promising start into the loose folds and pleats of a skirt or pair of trousers. In these cases the upper portion of the bottom is presented well, but the lower portion is rendered completely out of bounds and utterly isolated from interested observation.

The Waisted Curve

The thrilling meeting place of downward and upward curves is found in the neat concave tuck of body called the waistline. Now, admittedly, this place does not exist, in the obvious sense, for some people. For the majority, however, it does and it captures the eye and the hand of anyone studying curves. The waist is like a sudden intake of breath or a spontaneous change of direction which sets off the curve of bottom with magnificent grace.

The student should never be content to study the curve of waist from one angle alone, however. Rather, he or she should somehow view the waist from two to three perspectives in order to fully appreciate and enjoy the consequent slope of flesh into the ever-enticing bottom.

10. The Sunlight Factor

The youthful and all-too-innocent Princess Diana demonstrated to the world, a few years ago, just how effective a little sunlight can be at revealing hitherto hidden features. When a wily photographer asked her to pose with her back to the sun, she had no idea that the bright sunlight pierced her summer skirt with ease. The cruel result was that the photographer, and then the world, were given a perfect silhouette of the Princess's lower

Testing the Sunlight Factor at Home

anatomy. Bad luck for Her Highness, and a lesson to the rest of us on the power and truthfulness of sunlight.

In the science of clunology however, we cannot rely on such chance occurrences to provide us with study material. Yet, undoubtedly, sunlight has a crucial role to play and after several years of curriculum development its position in our studies has been defined. For purposes of privacy and convenience, those students who work and live in a non-sunny clime (such as the United Kingdom) may, instead of sunlight, use a 40,000 megawatt lightbulb fixed to a moveable metal arm.

In the tests that follow, the sun or lightbulb is made to shine directly on to the front of the clothed or unclothed subject who, by the way, should stand in a relaxed but upright manner. The student remains in a seated position directly behind the subject and observes the degree of sunlight penetration occurring at the juxtaposition of upper thighs and lower bottom. The results are qualified according to five major possible categories, as follows.

Not a Glimmer

The title of this category says it all: namely that, try as one might, it is impossible to find a single sliver of light penetrating the tight cluster of thigh and bottom. Both men and women can possess this feature, though it is likely that slightly more men than women do so. An expensive result of the Not A Glimmer factor is that the inner leg of trousers wears out in very little time. Women who are of the Not A Glimmer type and also wear nylon tights may suffer from 'thigh swish', an unfortunate sound which is clearly discernible at some distance caused by the nylon-clad thighs rubbing together. This has also been known to generate static electricity of such a high voltage that entire neighbourboods have been blacked out by a sudden surge of thigh activity.

Some benefits of this factor which are often over-looked, however, are that any Not a Glimmer owner – whether male or female – could probably earn lots of money as a wrestler with a speciality of crushing his or her opponent at the union of thigh and bottom. And for those who enjoy wearing skirts there is little need to wear an underslip.

The Distant Star

It is interesting how conjecture and discussion can cause an otherwise mundane topic to become mysterious and alluring. Yet precisely that phenomenon occurs when the Distant Star factor is observed for the first time. One's first reaction is to call in a colleague to confirm one's suspicions, which inevitably causes the discussion to begin and therefore the fascination and allure to grow and grow.

The Distant Star is a glimmer of light which thrusts confidently through the merest of openings in that same meeting place of upper thigh and lower bottom. Now, a glimmer is a shard of light of any size or intensity so it is easy to see that discussion might arise, in some circumstances, as to whether a glimmer exists at all. To prevent heated discussion, it is recommended that the student of the Sunlight Factor simply holds a mirror about twelve inches from the bottom. If a glimmer of light is penetrating, it will be reflected in a most definite fashion.

Most Distant Star factors are, in fact, quite obvious and the mirror expedient will not be necessary. But here we must mention an ancillary phenomenon which often occurs once a student spots a Distant Star: he or she has an irresistible urge to gently but unambiguously insert their index finger into this fleshy aperture. Mention is only made of this phenomenon because it so closely resembles a perverse act. In pressing one's finger into this opening, the sunlight is completely blocked and the factor is converted to a Not A Glimmer. Think for one minute of the story of the boy who put his finger in the dyke and you will recognise the similarity. In each case, one of nature's most powerful forces (water and sunlight) is controlled by a small finger in a small hole. Should the student clunologist feel this urge welling up within them they should leave the room immediately for a brief sojourn in some fresh air. This will prevent unfortunate misunderstandings, and alleviate the ever-present possibility of acts of perversity which it is the duty of professional clunologists to guard against. The price of free bums is, of course, eternal vigilance in this respect.

The Rising Sun

Here all need for mirrors, fingers and other devices is put aside. The Rising Sun is an obvious penetration of sunlight through a distinct opening created by the juxtaposition of upper thigh and lower bottom. The shape of this opening gives this category its name: the thighs meet a few centimetres below the union of pygal cheeks so that the emerging light appears like a morning sun peeking brightly through a mountain pass.

As this aperture is larger than either of the previous two described, the sunlight may seem, at first, somewhat dissipated. However, one or two of Professor Grimes' students have experimented with means of focusing this light with the use of magnifying glasses. One did this so successfully that he was able to use the resulting beam of light instead of matches to light his gas fire. The other student, after several attempts, was able to recharge all of her solar-powered batteries with one three-minute burst of the Rising Sun factor focused through a magnifying glass.

The Blazing Star

Most people, whether religiously-inclined or not, are familiar with the story of the three wise men following a bright star. And perhaps, too, you can call to mind the shape of this star, as often depicted on Christmas cards. These images are the inspiration for the name of this category, especially as the shape of the pygal Blazing Star is identical to the blazing star of the nativity. It is sharply diamond-shaped at the top with a very long, slender and pointed tail and is created by the delicate pout of pygal cheeks at the top; a soft, inward curve of the upper thighs to complete the diamond; then a long and gradual slope of thighs which postpone their meeting for several centimetres down the leg. This last feature causes the 'tail' effect which makes this category so distinctive and so instantly recognisable.

The Absolute Sunbeam

One could drive the proverbial coach and horses through the opening defined in this category. For here the buttocks barely pout, the thighs do not meet and daylight can be seen without interruption right down to the knees and, in many cases, the ankles. The result is a proper shaft of light, a total sunbeam: uninhibited, unwaylaid. An owner of an Absolute Sunbeam should not apply for work as a wrestler but may achieve some success as a teacher of waltzes, polkas and foxtrots – the knees of the student dancers having plenty of room for manoeuvre before collision occurs.

The Grimes Theory of Archetypes

Capitalising upon some initial work by Jung and others, but not fearing to tread where those others lost their nerve, Professor Grimes has given the world his 'Theory of Archetypes' which is, perhaps, his single greatest contribution to the entire field of clunology. It is equally relevant both to the layperson and the professional. For example, how many times (countless, no doubt) have you awoken from a vivid dream only to find that your partner or accomplice has also dreamt of *precisely the same bottom*? The Grimes theory can explain this, and much more resides, from the primitive bottom that cavemen used to draw on the walls of their outside lavatories, right up to the fashion-model of today's centre-fold. For Grimes has isolated ten basic Cluneal Archetypes, listed below. Read, learn and inwardly digest.

The Sumo

How fortunate that most people in the West have seen pictures of enormous Sumo wrestlers – this makes the task of explaining the parameters of this category so much easier. The Sumo bottom is characterised by its formidable nature, not necessarily sheer bulk. The buttocks are solid and heavy with occasional endearing dimples that hide a truly savage potential. In

Shakespeare's *A Midsummer Night's Dream*, Bottom was a character (fully Sumo-bottomed) who felt he could do everything *and* do it better than anyone else! People with this trait may turn out to be conceited, ignorant and socially lumbering. A quick study of the other dominating features of the Sumo bottom shows that it usually registers a Rising Orb profile and a definite Peaches Rear View. The cleavage is either Rainforest or Long, Thin Line and the Sway Factor is generally of the Collision variety. Curves of stomach and thigh rate high on the scale of curves with an extraordinarily high rating for size of curve. The Sunlight Factor is always a Not A Glimmer. Other characteristics, such as Wobble, Bounce and Tone, vary considerably from Sumo to Sumo and are not essential to the definition of this bottom. Sumo owners often have their own chair in their front room which is off limits to anyone else, including the cat. They frequently pick on smaller people (or countries) than themselves and may use their formidable size to smother and overwhelm. Gentle and humane Sumo do, however, exist. Famous owners of the Sumo bottom include Nero, Marquis de Sade and Queen Victoria.

The Kitty Cat

The owner of this bottom is a combination of fastidiousness and raunchiness which is evident in every street cat or pampered pussy on this earth. They have a tendency towards anality and precociousness which they incite in others by flaunting their tiny little tushes to all and sundry at the least excuse. The Kitty Cat profile is usually Flat; its Rear View is a definite Peanuts. When moving the Kitty Cat employs a Rolling Sway; when standing still there is a Blazing Star Sunlight Factor. The cleavage varies considerably, usually according to the sex of the owner, but tends to be either the Death Valley or the Touch and Go cleavage. Raisa Gorbachev, James Cagney and Cleopatra are excellent examples of this bottom: each of them wielding it with particular effect in their chosen fields of endeavour.

The Pug

These rather sturdy, muscular bottoms are recognisable by the jaunty swagger with which they are carried. This particular form of swagger is achieved using a combination of the Pivot Sway and round-the-clock Twopenny Piece clench. As you might expect, the precise shape of the buttocks is a combination of the Hillocks profile and the Peaches or Peanuts Rear View. Thus the twenty-four hour clench is made easy and, in time, becomes second nature to the owner of the Pug bottom.

Watch out for pictures of Humphrey Bogart, Charlie Chaplin and Karl Marx for proof that they are leaders in the Pug phenomenon. Their Convergent cleavages and Distant Star sunlight factors provide conclusive evidence that this self-satisfied category of bottoms is quietly thriving, often in California. Just like the puppy this category is named after, however, the Pug-bottomed may be quick to turn and tear at the ankles, knee-caps and etceteras of those around them. So take care when in their vicinity.

The Stork

Like all birds of the same name, the owner of a Stork bottom moves with a grace and slow easiness which belies their quick tongue, powerful wit and whippet-like strength. Thankfully they are usually merciful in their use of these attributes. This bottom is the peaceful resolution atop extremely long legs and retains a functional appearance most of the time.

Salvador Dali and Aubrey Beardsley are prime examples of the Stork bottom. Each possesses the deceptive quick-slow style of movement and conservation which a Stork uses to keep their audience on guard. Their Lumbar Sway may cause them problems in later life, but most Stork owners learn this early in their adulthood and take remedial steps. The other characteristics of the Stork bottom are a Flat profile with an indisputable Death Valley cleavage; an Acorns or Pears Rear View and an Absolute Sunbeam sunlight factor. These attributes commune to assist the dark-horse personality of the be-Storked.

The Nipper

Spot an over-dressed, attention-seeking person with an obviously pouting bottom, or lower lip, and you may have happened upon a Nipper. This category of bottom is sported by John Travolta, Pablo Picasso and Gary Hart and its features include an Acorn rear view and a Tear-drop or Low-slung profile. The Touch and Go cleavage hints at some of the chronic reticence of Nipper owners, who may turn out to be very insecure people.

They possess much that is lovable in their personalities, however. They will usually try anything at least once and they won't necessarily keep their exploits to themselves. You may not think this is lovable at first, but in fact they use this attribute to provide endless hours of amusing entertainment to millions of people. Also lovable is the rare and beautiful Rising Sun sunlight factor (it of the inserted finger fame) which graces this bottom. No wonder John became famous for saying 'Ah! Ah! Ah! Ah!' Most Nipper owners should be told to hide their knicker lines.

The Destroying Angel

Also known as The Fiend, this bottom is a powerhouse of pent-up strength and emotion. Usually belonging to sexual athletes or passional Platonists, this category of bottom emits a subtle warning to all who come close to guard against sudden contact – *unless* they are able to take the consequences. Consider for a moment the modern-day owners of Destroying Angel bottoms and you may begin to understand the importance of this observation.

Judy Garland, Clark Gable and Bing Crosby are three of the more famous owners, each of whose calm, slinky passage through the corridors of Hollywood is peppered with the explosive rat-tat-tats of their destructive force. An attentive student can see the potential: the apparent harmlessness of the Hillock profile, the Peaches rear view, the Convergent cleavage and the Not A Glimmer sunlight factor could lull one into careless camaraderie. It is the gait which reveals the real menace. The confident Rolling Sway betrays the slightly higher than expected ratings in both Bounce and Lift before it shudders, in a split second, to become a Collision Sway. Obviously the right time to high-tail your way into the distance.

The Celestial

Whoever coined the phrase 'Heaven on Earth' knew something about bottoms. Not that this category of bottom is necessarily heavenly, rather it aspires to the heaven-grown point of view. Owners of this bottom are forever forgetting their earthly attachments and pursuing ethereal and entirely honourable channels of communication. Some succeed, it is true, others fail dismally without knowing it, all have the Celestial sign written clearly across their derrières.

The Celestial bottom is often left unattended and uncared for and, at times, this can cause the owner to forget it is there and so use it in what seems like a furtive manner. This is, of course, a misunderstanding. If the owner could only be made more aware of the character and inner qualities of his or her bottom, theirs would become a whole, aware bottom. Woody Allen, Shirley Maclaine and Michael J. Fox each possess a Celestial rear which, it must be said, are in excellent condition. The same cannot be said for all Celestials.

The Flat or Tear-drop profile of a standard Celestial needs regular attention to avoid complete deterioration. Similarly, the Touch and Go or Death Valley cleavage needs regular oiling to make sure it does not become unduly creased or otherwise blemished. Little can be done to alter the Absolute Sunbeam that is usual to this bottom, though some exercises may be done to alter the size of the bottom to suit this sunlight factor. The Celestial is often either a Peanuts or Bunches of Grapes rear view. In other words, one extreme or the other on the scale of size and shape. Most owners of Celestial bottoms have matured into the realisation that they were given this Rear View in order that they become aware of both their bottom and their celestial calling.

The Demon Bunny

Think of Fidel Castro, James Dean and King Henry VIII in order to initiate your understanding of the Demon Bunny bottom. All of these men are real tough guys, when they want to be, and big softies the rest of the time. So it is with this category of bottom. It is the ultimate in toughness and demonhood in that rather definite, slightly overstated condition we all look for in toughness and demonhood. Yet it is also perfectly ordinary and unthreatening. The profile is hugely Hillocked, the rear view is a perfect Peaches. The fierce Rainforest or Convergent cleavage and the welcoming Rising Sun factor combine so well that, by the end of our observation, we are wondering where the Demon is.

Such is the essence of this most adaptable rump. Its features seem so well suited to one another, so subtle and unobtrusive that we forget that therein lies its double-character. For the owner of this bottom can spring into action within a split second to overwhelm and subvert an opponent and then be back in a rocking chair reading fairy tales the next. The Demon Bunny owner is extremely responsive: to love, fear, anger, compassion; and extremely expressive as well: always capable of and willing to display whatever is necessary to achieve a satisfactory outcome in the task they have set themselves.

The Gas Bag

Some people still consider the bottom to be an area of taboo as well as a possible source of embarrassment. These people nevertheless want to receive all the sensations and rewards a bottom can provide – so they just get everyone else to do the hard work for them. Strangely enough, owners of this category of bottom can often be found in the same line of work. Here are three examples of proper Gas Bag bottomed people: George Bush, Ollie North, P. W. Botha.

Each of these owners possesses an archetypal Gas Bag bottom as noted by the fact that they all have Low-slung profiles with Bunches of Grapes rear views, Long, Thin Line cleavages and Blazing Star sunlight factors. This combination of features is the only way they can get other people to kiss, lick, flatter or spank their prudish posteriors while *they* pretend none of it is happening.

Digestive disturbances, including anal eructations, are common to the owners of the Gas Bag bottom who seem unable to keep themselves from performing these attention-seeking stunts. In fact, so used are they to using their bottoms instead of the rest of their personalities to get their own way, that they are often mistaken for ass-holes and forced into compromising and sometimes damaging positions.

The Gibbon

Like its bright and attractive namesake, the Gibbon bottom is a revelation of contrasting characteristics. The profile is a Rising Orb, but the rear view is a Peanuts. The cleavage is a definite Death Valley, but the sunlight factor is a distinct Rising Sun. Do not let this combination confuse you, however. Quite simply, this bottom illustrates an owner who lives by very sharply drawn lines.

The lines are not necessarily moral, straight or even comprehensible – they are simply sharply drawn. Which makes many Gibbon-bottomed people seem very ruthless and sometimes even savage. At the very least they are considered practical, in the meaning of the word that precludes almost every other quality except practicality. Three of the most famous Gibbon owners are Imelda Marcos, John Wayne and Little Bo Peep.

And so we come to the end of this summary outline of the skills involved in bottom spotting. Each talent, skill and technique has been touched upon only briefly due to lack of space, so it is reliant upon the aspiring bottom spotter to indulge him or herself in the time and energy needed to fully develop each area of expertise. Should you wish to continue, and become a qualified, professional clunologist, you must complete the exercises and achievements outlined in the remainder of this book and spend at least ten years becoming proficient in each and every one of them.

3

CHERISH THAT BOTTOM!

The bottom is rarely pampered in the same extravagant way as are more public parts of the human anatomy, such as the face and hands. Yet, considering the vital role the rear end plays in health, mobility and sexual attraction, it deserves at least as much attention and consideration as the face and hair. Unfortunately, most of us have no idea at all of how to make the most of what we've got – it certainly isn't included in the 'what every mother should tell her children' package handed down through the generations. This chapter will solve the problem and introduce the mysteries of bottom beautification in a way that is easily understood and achieved. For, although somewhat inaccessibly situated, the bottom is still within the reach of all but the most corpulent owner. So don't let down your rear guard: learn to reach back and cherish!

Giving Due Care and Attention

The first step on the way to creating a loved and beautified bottom is to have a look at what you've got. And the first step on the way to looking at what you've got is to remove all of your lower-body clothing. Although this may, at first, seem a childish or somewhat silly thing to do, you will notice a feeling of relief and lightheartedness immediately you do it. This sensation harks back to the early days of humanity, when to be other than gleeful when naked was unheard of. So relax and let yourself be a part of the bigger picture.

Next, you must arrange to stand with your back to a large mirror (a three-leaved mirror, if possible) while, at the same time, holding a hand mirror in front and slightly to one side of your face. This arrangement of looking glasses will enable you to study your bottom without having to twist uncomfortably round or peer out of the corner of your eye. Take this opportunity to note the unique characteristics of your bottom and, if you like, assess these according to the guidelines issued in the previous chapter. Of most importance, however, is the use of this private time as a means of becoming acquainted with your bottom. Some people experience a profound release of pent up tension when they first clap eyes on their own derrière, often describing the event as 'restorative', 'cathartic' or even 'uplifting'. Psychologists have long attributed this effect to the realisation of acceptability – a feeling of 'my bottom's as good as anyone else's bottom'. There is also an element of having finished the jigsaw of one's own self-image: knowing, at last, what one looks like from the rear! Let's not spend too long on this essentially private experience, however. Enough to say that you should enjoy the experience, repeat it as often as you like and make notes, drawings or spontaneous remarks while looking at your reflected bottom.

The next step is to gradually clothe your bottom again. Start with knickers and have a good look at what those knickers really do – or don't do – for your pygal prominences. If you own more than one style of nether-garment, try them on in succession, finally selecting the pair that *add* to your bottom's beauty. Professor Grimes has received hundreds of letters over the years from people who have discovered that this simple expedient has revived lack-lustre love lives and strengthened the bond between husband and wife. Specifically, the removal of two-tone Y-fronts and poorly-styled bikini-cut panties from the marital wardrobe creates scope for the partnered bottoms to rediscover their original attraction.

After the knickers, the dressing process continues with an ever attentive view to the rear. But it is not the purpose of this book to define fashion and re-stock your wardrobe, it is enough to say that, having become acquainted with your botty once again, you are less likely to encase it in ugly or confining attire. It is up to you to maintain this attitude of care and attention and, to check that you aren't slipping, it is suggested that you simply repeat your study of your nude nethers on a regular basis. Now, let us return to our discussion of how to care for the essential bottom.

The bottoms of poetry are usually described as silky, downy places that are irresistibly soft. This description is true of the ideal, well-cared for bottom but, sadly, far from true of the majority of unattended rumps. Often the flesh is goose-pimpled, coarse, dry and spotty for no other reason than the owner does not consider his or her behind worthy of attention. Be forewarned! If you have one of these abhorrent, repellent bottoms, pledge now to do your utmost to salvage its inherent beauty from the pits of neglect.

Oils

A daily oiling of the bottom will do wonders to revive the silky softness you enjoyed as a babe. This project may be carried out by yourself or a friend or spouse and is best performed immediately after bathing, while the body is still slightly damp. Although the technique described is specific to the natal region, you should realise that the whole body will undoubtedly benefit from a similar treatment.

Select an oil that is vegetable-derived (do not use butter, lard or other animal fats no matter how much you may be tempted) and either pure or lightly scented with natural oils. Oils from the sesame, almond, peach kernel and hazel nut are all excellent choices to start with and each of these may be enhanced with aromatic plant oils such as rose, orange or lavender. Pour the oil into a small, shallow dish and dip your three middle fingers into it. Immediately rest the oily fingers at the top of your cluneal cleavage, letting the oil run freely down the cleavage for a few seconds. Now, using both hands, begin to rub the oil into the skin of the cleavage with a vertical motion. Give especial attention to the top of the cleavage, at the small of your back, as this area is often chafed by bedding and tight-fitting clothing.

Dip your fingers into the oil as soon as you feel the skin tugging under the rubbing movement. If possible, dip both sets of fingers into the oil for the next stage in this resuscitative process. At once, place your fingers at the very top and to the outer edge of each buttock. Let the oil run off your fingers onto the buttocks, then begin the rubbing movement. Using the flat of your hand, rub the oil slightly up and outwards from the centre of each buttock. Use considerable pressure and gradually increase the size and span of these oil strokes until you are making a broad, crescent-shaped movement. Once again, dip your fingers into the oil.

This time, press your fingers onto the outer edge of each buttock. This area is often rough with goose-flesh or chafed skin so you should begin the rubbing with a small, circular movement directly over these areas. Gradually broaden the circle and add a downward and slightly inward movement to it. Continue for several seconds until the oil is well distributed. dip your fingers in the oil one final time.

Place your oily fingers at the lowest point of each buttock and begin, immediately, to rub the oil in a circular, lifting motion. The circular movement ensures that the portion of the buttock which is actually sat upon is well oiled; the lifting movement stimulates circulation and makes sure that the very centre of each buttock has not been overlooked in this most pleasurable caring process. If possible, spend the next five minutes resting, keeping warm by wrapping up in a dressing gown. Repeat the oiling daily.

Powders

There are two reasons for powdering your bottom, each with quite separate goals. In the first, a lightly perfumed, skin-toned powder is generously applied to the upper cleavage and the small of the back with the occasional foray, on a pouting bottom, to the underside of each buttock (often called 'the crease'). A soft brush is the best means of applying powder in this way as it is quick, effective and also more than somewhat congenial. The purpose of this activity is to maintain an even skin tone in those who tend to perspire heavily in these regions.

Due to their tendency towards hirsute haunches, prolific perspirers are usually men (even the most macho of men will enjoy and benefit from this little beauty routine). Of course, women can make good use of this form of powdering, too. Strippers, for instance, or semi-nude dancers will find this little trick an invaluable enhancement to the visual impact of their routine. Although the aim of this powdering is to make the bottom appear natural and untouched, most of those who powder in this way claim that they feel more attractive and responsive as a result – even when their bottoms are tucked away inside layers of clothing. The powder may be applied oneself or by a friend or spouse.

The second form of powdering is done for purely non-practical reasons. Both men and women enjoy this practice, though very hairy-bottomed men may find that it is difficult to achieve an acceptable result. Briefly, the buttocks are studied in both their relaxed and clenched state before a blush-coloured powder is applied. This form of powdering is best performed by a friend or spouse, though selection of the colour of blusher may be a joint activity. The style of application is entirely open-ended and, like in face make-up, should enhance the unique characteristics of the bottom in question. A feeling of increased attractiveness and heightened receptivity is reported by virtually everyone who enjoys this form of powdering.

Paints

Bottom-painting is almost exclusively performed for thrills – there are only rare occasions when it could be performed for any practical reason (British Members of Parliament and South African state police excepted). For instance, it may be resorted to as a means of hiding a blemish or scar and, in these cases, a subtle application of standard face make-up is always the rule. At all other times, bottom painting is a diverting way of spending a few hours. The single prohibitive rule is that only non-toxic body paints or make-up should be used. Otherwise, the painting process is left for you to make of it what you wish. The paintings may be abstract, humorous, stimulating or purposeful in some way.

Most people who paint find it one of the best ways of becoming really familiar with a bottom, while those being painted claim to greatly enjoy the delicate sensations associated with it.

It is, of course, not possible to leave the subject of bottom painting without recounting two near-legendary tales which Professor Grimes mentions in an early but still definitive work on the subject (*Pygal Pigmentation Ancient and Modern*, Strict Books, 1955). The first concerns a huge-and-hairy-bottomed man who, invited to a bottom painting party, found that no one could paint his bottom because of his hirsuteness. His frustration became so great that he went into the toilet to cut his wrists but, instead, decided to put the razor to better use. He emerged from the toilet with a razor, shaving cream and towel and challenged the prettiest woman at the party to shave his buttocks. She was delighted at the novelty of his suggestion, shaved his bottom of all hair except areas designed as eyebrows, moustache and beard then proceeded to paint in the missing features to create an excellent facsimile of Karl Marx. The man and the woman were, by all accounts, so taken with one another by the end of the evening that they eventually married and continued to hold shave 'n' paint parties for many years.

The second case history comes from the yearbook of an American high school located in remotest Wyoming. According to the printed account (verified by police records of the time), a group of boisterous high school seniors became disgruntled when they were expelled from one of the town's Ice Cream Socials. Eager to wreak their revenge on the townspeople, in particular the mayor's wife – a stuffy and overbearing woman who interfered in everyone's business – the young students drove recklessly away in a large black sedan.

After some discussion, one of the students came up with the idea of mooning the Ice Cream Social. All the students agreed but one offered the further suggestion that they paint their nudity to increase the effect. With speed and precision the bottoms were painted to resemble the congressmen, senators and the governor of the state. When, some time later, the large, black sedan car cruised slowly past the park in which the Social was being held, more than one of the townspeople proclaimed that they had seen the governor. When this news reached the mayor's wife, she immediately bullied her way forward to be the first to welcome him. At her approach the black car pulled over and a deep voice called authoritatively to her 'Could you possibly offer me one of those ice cream cones?' The mayor's wife grabbed one from the hands of a nearby child and held it out to the governor, from whom the voice had seemed to emerge. 'Put it in my mouth, please' the voice said. The mayor's wife dutifully thrust the ice cream cone into the gaping mouth of the strange looking governor. Only at this moment did the truth become apparent. The mooning students emerged, hysterically, from the car – one, the governor, with an ice cream cone affixed to his lower cluneal cleavage. All further Ice Cream Socials were cancelled for that summer, the mayor resigned and the enterprising students left for university and greater fame.

Perfumes

It must be mentioned that a touch of perfume may be all that is necessary to lift a bottom from obscurity. The suggestion is (particularly aimed at men with 'Rainforest' cleavages) that a dab of your favourite cologne or aftershave placed at the apex of your cluneal cleavage will do wonders for your sense of attractiveness. Women may position their favourite scent in the same place if they wish, or in the crease between lower buttock and upper thigh for a longer-lasting scent. Both men and women experience an increase in both appeal and appetite as a result of this considerate action.

Cleavage Enhancers

What's good enough for the bosom is good enough for the bottom. Not least in the area of cleavage enhancers. In these days of mini-kinis and posing pouches, of sun-worshipping and nudist beaches, the cluneal cleavage receives at least as much exposure as the mammary cleavage. So why not give it equal care and attention?

All of the previous caring procedures could be said to, in some way, enhance the cleavage. But there are more specific steps that may be taken. The first is to wear swimwear or knickers that will grip the buttocks in such a way as to promote or emphasise the cleavage. These items of clothing are not necessarily comfortable in all situations, but they are effective in making the cleavage larger and deeper, at least temporarily.

Secondly, the use of eye-liner pencils and highlighters to draw in a cleavage where only a minute one exists may turn a shallow, shadowless cleavage into a deep, curvaceous one. Choose from a very wide range of colours and practise a light hand at first to come up with just the right shape and colour tone. And be sure to alter the style of your cleavage make-up to suit the lighting and the time of day.

Becoming Expert at Finger Flattery

Everyone loves to know that their bottom is looking good and dressed well, but undoubtedly, the greatest thrill of all comes from having your bottom touched in a caring manner. In fact, most people will go to great lengths to have their bottom stroked, rubbed, caressed or fondled. And why not? It is a very sensitive, personal area which, though also notoriously near to the more grossly explicitly sexual anatomy, is capable of eliciting a great deal of sensual delight all by itself. Here are a few methods by which such delight may be achieved.

To ensure success with these techniques, it is essential that you assume a mental attitude of wishing to flatter the bottom in hand (as Professor Grimes puts it, 'End Zen'). However much you are tempted to think of your own desires and outlandish cravings at this special moment, it is absolutely essential for you to control your mind and cultivate an attitude of flatternisation. Then, and only then, will the strokes, pinches, grips, bites, clawings etc which follow successfully create pleasure in your friend and therefore yourself. Flatternisation is achieved by imagining that every touch of the tush is a communication and that every such communication will be returned to you in equal measure.

Strokes

These forms of flattery are gentle, soft movements using the fingertips or flats of the hands against the buttocks. There are as many different styles of stroking as there are people; however, five of the most basic forms are outlined here. In each method, the owner of the bottom about to be stroked should stretch out, face down, on a comfortable bed or carpet while the person about to stroke should kneel or sit beside them. All strokes should be performed so that there is a minimum amount of friction and the maximum amount of nerve stimulation.

Circling the Globes: the fingertips of both hands are placed at the meeting of lower buttock and upper thigh. From here, they are drawn gently up along the line of the cleavage at which point the two sets of fingers part and stroke softly in an outward direction over the top of the cheeks. The stroke continues down the outer edge of the cheeks, inward along the crease of the buttocks and finally meeting again at their starting position. This motion may be repeated several times.

Mountain Climbing: the fingers of both hands are spread widely apart and placed along the outer edge of their respective cheeks. Then, with a very slight fluttering motion of the fingers, the fingers are drawn inward towards the summit of each buttock. They are then lifted away from the buttocks, replaced at the outer edge of each buttock and the movement is repeated.

Running the Ridge: the fingers of each hand are held together and placed at the lower edge of each buttock, so that the palm of the hand faces towards the owner's head. The fingers are then pulled gently up along the ridge of each cheek until they reach the small of the back. The starting position is resumed and the movement is repeated. The pressure of fingers upon cheeks may be varied considerably in this stroke.

Tickling the Cleavage: one or both sets of fingers may be used for this stroke. The fingers are placed at the apex of the cleavage then drawn very gently down the length of the cleavage. Here they circle the meeting place of lower buttock and upper thigh before being drawn gently up the cleavage to the apex again. The stroker should ensure that the owner of the bottom is content with the degree of downward/inward pressure being exerted; any adjustments should be made without delay.

Cheeky Creases: the fingers of both hands are placed together at the meeting place of lower buttock and upper thigh, with the palms of each hand facing outward toward the hip. The fingers are then drawn gently but swiftly outward along the cluneal crease. The fingers are repositioned in their starting place and the movement is repeated several times.

Rubs

These forms of flattery are performed using as much or as little of the hands and fingers as necessary, according to the effect desired. Also, the amount of pressure exerted differs greatly from that of stroking, as does the speed and rhythm of each movement. Rubs are also called 'massage' by many people, with the rubbers called 'masseurs' and the rubbed called 'clients' or 'punters'. Either terminology will do.

During any rubbing session, the person being rubbed should relax their buttocks as thoroughly as possible, find a comfortable resting position and leave the rest to nature. The person doing the rubbing should also make him or herself comfortable at all times to ensure a sincere and effective rub. Oil or talcum powder may be used, if desired, to prevent excessive friction between the skin of hand and bottom.

Finger-tip Kneading: the wrists of the hands are lifted so that the fingers rest in a downward direction – much like the position assumed before playing scales on the piano. The fingers are held as though they were holding a small egg and then pressed firmly into the flesh of each buttock. Wherever they are on the buttock, the fingers maintain a kneading motion and a firm downward pressure. The fingers may extend to knead a very broad area, but they should never reduce in extent beyond the initial egg-size. The firm downward pressure is intended to benefit the gluteal muscles, lying beneath the thick layer of pygal fat. This can have a very soothing and health-giving effect.

Thick Pinch 'n' Pull: using one or both hands, the rubber pinches a thick layer of tushy tissue between thumb and fingers and pulls it unambiguously outward or upward. The sensation to be achieved in the person being rubbed is a mixture of mild discomfort, tickling and deep curiosity about what will happen next. The pinched 'n' pulled tissue may be wobbled briefly while still in the pulled position, if the owner is endowed with sufficient flesh.

Strong-finger Rotation: after exploring the gluteal region, the rubber uses either a knuckle or a strong, straight finger to press very firmly and deeply onto a single point in the bottom. Once the proper depth is reached, the knuckle or finger is slowly rotated or wriggled from side to side. This is a remedial movement which can relax large areas of muscle tissue, relieve pain and prevent nerve and muscle spasm. It is used, also, as a means of creating deep relaxation in the person being rubbed.

Big Squeeze: the fingers of both hands are spread as far as possible, then one hand is placed on each buttock. The fingers are drawn firmly together so that a great deal of the buttock is squeezed into each hand. This squeeze is maintained for several seconds and the handful may, if both parties are agreed, be moved in a circular direction to enhance the sensations which accompany a squeeze of this size. The rubber may emit growling sounds if this seems natural to them and appropriate to the situation.

Slow Drag: the fingers or palms of each hand (depending on the position of the rubber) are placed firmly against the crease of each buttock. Then, exerting a great deal of pressure upon each buttock, the fingers or hands are dragged along the ridge of the buttocks until they reach the small of the back. The movement is slow and sure and may be repeated several times.

Lifting the Tone a Bit

Much has been said recently of the magnificent changes achieved in the shape and tone of some of the world's most famous bottoms. And, although some of these changes may have been helped along with the aid of a surgeon's scalpel, many were achieved by hard work and perseverance on the part of the owner. You see, a good bottom needs good musculature and good musculature can only be maintained by using the muscles of the bottom. Here is a small collection of exercises, movements and tips which will help you to develop gluteals you can gloat over.

Exercises

Put on some soothing or beaty music, take off your clothes and give your bottom ten minutes each day all to itself.

Isometric Toning: sit or stand and tighten your gluteal muscles as much as possible. Hold this tightened position for ten seconds, then relax the muscles again. Wait five seconds, then repeat the clenching movement and hold for ten seconds again. Repeat in this way a further ten times. Repeat the whole exercise later in the day.

Prone Leg Lift: lie on your stomach and cross your hands under your forehead, so that your elbows rest out to your sides. Spread your feet about twelve inches apart and press the front of your pelvis firmly into the floor (you should feel pressure on the two bones at the front of your hips). Keep these bones in contact with the floor, stretch one leg and then slowly raise it a little distance off the floor. Hold it briefly in that position, then slowly lower it to the floor in a controlled fashion. Rest, then repeat the movement with the other leg. To increase the effects of this exercise you may: increase the length of time you hold your leg lifted, increase the number of times you can perform it, or raise both legs off the floor at once. The gluteal muscles are toned as a result of this exercise.

Ham Stretch: stand with both knees bent and fold your upper body down so that you can easily touch your fingers to the floor. Let the top of your head aim at the floor, so that your face is looking directly behind you. Now lift your tail-bone towards the ceiling: to do this you will have to straighten your legs somewhat. Hold the position you achieve for five seconds then fold your legs again and relax briefly. Repeat the exercise six times before coming slowly into a standing position once again. This exercise will stretch the muscles along the backs of your thighs and into your buttocks, thus improving the exact location and lift of your buttocks.

Walking: Walking is one of the best forms of exercise yet invented for maintaining and improving gluteal glamour. This is hardly surprising when you recall that it was walking which gave us our prominent peaches in the first place. An absolute minimum of three hours' brisk walking each week is needed to keep a healthy, happy bottom. And if you can spend some of that time walking up a slope or hill, so much the better for your bottom and the health of your lower back. If this sounds like a lot of time, think again: most of us can walk three miles per hour without trying. Make sure you wear comfortable shoes when walking.

Swimming: the breast and side strokes especially provide a real challenge to your gluteal muscles. If you are fortunate and have easy access to a pool, try these strokes for a total of fifteen minutes each day, four to five days a week. Otherwise, swim when you can and combine it with walking and a good routine of other exercises.

Movements

There are some movements which most of us do not consider exercises but which can, nevertheless, help us improve the tone of our buttock muscles.

Belly Dance Movement: this is as it sounds and can be performed by men and women alike for life-long health and happiness. The buttocks aren't the only parts this movement reaches, however: lower back, abdomen, thighs and hips are also benefactors. To perform it, stand with your feet at least eighteen inches apart and your knees bent. Now circle your pelvis so that your tailbone moves back, to one side, forward, to the other side, then back again in a continuous movement. Relax your breathing as you move and try the circling motion in both directions. When you have got the knack of it, you may speed it up or perform it to music. In any case, repeat the circle at least eight times in each direction.

Sitting Tall: if sitting on a chair, such as an office chair, ensure that both feet are flat on the floor in front of you and that your back is tall and straight. If sitting on the floor, let your knees rest out to your sides and lengthen your spine so you are sitting tall and straight. Whichever position you hold, stretch the muscles in your lower back and buttocks by moving gently backwards and forwards. Keep your back straight at all times and repeat often.

Standing Tilt: when speaking on the telephone, waiting in a queue or any other time when you must stand for a length of time, ease the sense of fatigue and discomfort in the bottom and lower back with this movement. Bend your knees very slightly then tilt your pelvis backwards and forwards so that your tailbone moves forward under you, then back behind you. Let your gluteal muscles tighten on each forward movement and relax on each backward movement.

Tips

Here is a selection of miscellaneous yet helpful hints and tips, drawn from a lifetime's experience of teaching, surveying and interviewing people on everything to do with the bottom:

* 'If you are a woman with a really uncontrollably wobbly bottom, don't wear heels any higher than 2½ inches. Otherwise

you will be showing off all that's worst about your rear!' (submitted by Angela W., Beauty Therapist)

* 'Men with flat, tiny bottoms should not wear shoes with metal inserts on the heels. Everyone thinks you're a real tight-ass if you do and women will think they will have to pay for the meal if you invite them for a date. P.S. I used to have a spotty bottom but now I eat one pound (445g) of aduki beans each week and my bottom is completely unspotted.' (submitted by Vera C., Secretary)

* 'Whenever you agree to massage a friend's bottom, ask your friend to go soak his or her bottom in the bath for five minutes so that it gets really warm and clean. Meanwhile, you should warm your fingers under the tap so you don't freeze the poor person into a state of posterior petrification.' (submitted by James F., Trainee Masseur)

* 'If you see goose-flesh forming on your thighs or bottom, cut down on the amount of sugar you eat and watch it disappear within a fortnight!' (submitted by Catherine W., Housewife)

* 'I used to suffer from a cold botty until I discovered the loofa. Now I use the loofa to give my bottom a real rubbing down for two minutes after each bath. And, guess what, no chilly cheeks!' (submitted by Sally P., Actress)

* 'I used to have a cold bottom all the time. Then I decided to fight fire with fire or, in this case, cold with cold. I immerse my bottom in a big bucket of cold water for three minutes every night. Then I rub myself dry, hop into bed and sleep warm and contented all night. Now my wife is not afraid to cuddle up to me.' (submitted by Frank D., Plasterer)

* 'I was nearly fired from my job as a cleaner because I never polished the brass handrails that run up four flights of stairs in the posh building where I work. My husband came up with the perfect solution and now I wrap polishing cloths round my bottom and slide down the railings to polish their tops. To polish underneath, I walk with a slow wriggle up the stairs again, with my bottom under the railing. I am fitter than

I've ever been and my husband thinks I'm wonderful.' (submitted by Jean H., Industrial Cleaner)

* 'A few months ago I noticed I was getting a bit broad in the beam – probably from too much sitting. I work in an office block of nine stories so I decided to do myself a favour and lose my lump. Now, whenever I am called to a meeting on another floor, I walk up and down the stairs. That goes for getting to my own office (on the seventh floor) every morning as well. All that climbing has improved my stamina *and* I am comfortable in my old trousers again.' (submitted by John M., Business Analyst)

* 'I have a bottom with a mind of its own! I do my best to keep it to a reasonable size and shape but, sometimes, it just seems to lose all of its dignity and get huge and horrible. I found the solution, though, and it really works! Once a month I go into the photocopying room at work, lock the door and lie down on the A3 copier. Then I take a photocopy of my bottom, roll it up and take it home where I pin it up on the door to my wardrobe. Nothing is more effective at keeping me in line and it in shape!' (submitted by Mandy P., Receptionist)

* 'After I turned forty, I began to notice the skin on my bottom was getting a little loose. I am not normally a vain man, but my wife commented on it, so I thought I should take some remedial action. After trying a number of ointments and exercises, I came upon an article about face masks in one of my wife's magazines. So I decided to try a bottom mask! In fact, I made up my own recipe, as follows:

Ingredients:
whites of 3 eggs
1 teaspoon honey
1 teaspoon olive oil
pinch of paprika

Method:
Begin to beat the egg whites in a large bowl and gradually add the remaining ingredients. Continue beating the egg whites

until they have reached the stiff peak stage. Apply to the entire bottom and remain still for 15 minutes. Wash well and repeat in one week's time.

I have found this very effective in toning my skin and making it feel soft and luxurious again. The paprika is especially good in winter, because it improves the circulation to the buttocks. P.S. Can one contract salmonella poisoning through openings in the skin?' (submitted by Rodney F., Accountant)

Cherishing Through the Ages

You can see that care and attention to the bottom is an essential activity for the whole and happy person. And it is a strange thing but care given is as rewarding and pleasurable as care received, as any owner of a cherished bottom will tell you. Another delightful aspect of this wonderful activity is that it can be a part of your life no matter what your age. It can take up a few minutes each day or several hours each week (cherishing activities make the ideal replacement for boring old television watching), and it can be enjoyed for no more than a few pennies' expense each week. Cherishing the bottom, one's own and that of others, is to truly acknowledge the dignity and beauty we, as humans, gained by standing and walking upright – thus creating for ourselves the ever glorious rump.

4

THE HALL OF FAME

The Ten Top Tushes of All Time

While it is clearly a grievously difficult task to select the ten most distinguished rear ends for this ultimate honour, there is one person – and one person only – whose years of diligent, assiduous study have prepared him for this most onerous of duties. Professor Geronimus L. Grimes (who else?) is such a man – in fact, the *only* man fit to undertake such a herculean, super-human endeavour. 'I am open to the beauty and grace within each and every bottom' he modestly wrote when accepting this grave duty. 'I have always had a natural tendency to be tolerant and optimistic in this way, something which was greatly encouraged and reinforced by my early public-school education. So you will understand that it is difficult for me to select specific bottoms and label them "best" or "most beautiful" or any other qualitative title. In the same breath I must say that we all need pygal heroes, prototypes, even archetypes to hold up and by which we may assess our own qualities.'

It is with ineffable pleasure, then, that we present for your inspiration, encouragement and ecstasy the results of Professor Grimes's long and traumatic deliberations. For he has succeeded in choosing a truly exemplary range of bottoms which have transcended the work-a-day bonds of normalcy to become famous and distinctive in their own right; bottoms which epitomise the profound degree of cluneal beauty which, with much hard work, it is possible to attain. But gentle reader, do not despair if you do not see our own bottom included here. Perhaps no photographs exist of it, yet. The way is long, the path is exceedingly narrow, but not impossible. Given time, care and attention, almost anyone may ascend to the pinnacles of posteriors that follow . . .

Now turn to the picture section.

5

THE HALL OF SHAME

Ten Tattered, Tasteless Tails

Hetty Bumslinger, the near-legendary German post-Freudian existentialist and director of the Baden-Baden Centre of Corrective Clunology put it neatly when she wrote in her *magnum opus, Spanking Is Not Enough: Angst, Anxiety and Anal Retention* (Boffo Book Club, Berlin, mail order only): 'some bottoms are born to beauty, some achieve beauty, other bottoms miss the boat entirely'. How true. Indeed, a bottom does not have to be woefully neglected or overgrown in order to be considered déclassé. The pertest posterior in the world may, on occasion, and if not properly preened, be considered to be so poorly presented that it positively precludes pygal pulchritude. Such are the rumps in this section of our pictorial survey of the rear end.

As in so many other fields of human endeavour, presentation is everything. While not everybody is fortunate enough to be endowed with the perfect posterior, we can all, nay we are *obliged*, to make the most of what we've got. And that includes not permitting our rear ends to be photographed when looking anything less than one hundred per cent.

It is, therefore, fellow clunologists, with some trepidation that we present the visual essay which follows. Under no circumstances should the various poses and decorations you will see be imitated at home. Or anywhere else, for that matter. We include them here merely as a warning against the photographic abuse of the bottom, and also as a spur to greater things, in the hope that their owners will, in future, strive to achieve for their bottoms that inner sense of beauty which makes such an emphatic and palpable difference to the cluneal charisma.

Now turn to the picture section.

6

THE CLUNOLOGY QUIZ

As you will be aware from reading this modest folio, the study of bottoms is a fascinating and genuine pursuit, worthy of a deep and life-long commitment. Now, to further stimulate your interest in the subject, here is a wide selection of questions for you and your partner or friends to answer. Many questions will provoke in-depth discussion and ponderous thought, others may incite laughter and further displays of mirth. Answers to some questions may be found in the pages of this book, other questions may require you to take your studies into the field or engage in library research for yourself. However you approach this quiz and however long it takes you to complete, by using it you will gain expertise and acumen as you pursue the ever-present bottom through the corridors of knowledge and experience. Good luck, and may the Bottom be with you!

1) In which film did Jane Fonda first reveal her rear end?
   a) *On Golden Pond*
   b) *Barbarella*
   c) *California Suite*

2) Summer holidays take you to Venice, most romantic of cities and spiritual home of the clunesvellicist (Bottom-pincher). While coming out of St Mark's Cathedral you receive a sudden and decisive tweak, but the crowd is too dense to allow you to turn round and confront the perpetrator. Do you:
   a) Instinctively scream blue murder at the top of your voice

b) Take it as a compliment – after all, this is what you came to Italy for, isn't it?
c) Get into the spirit of the thing and give the rump in front a playful tweak too

3) Which of the following is *not* a bottom-word?
a) Tush
b) Jacksey-pardy
c) Ears

4) You have successfully completed your studies in clunology and are now a registered clunologist. You decide to practise from your home. How will you list your practice in the Yellow Pages?
a) Acme Bottom Company
b) The Bottom Clinic
c) Gluteal Assessment Practitioner

5) What does the abbreviation BLT *really* stand for?
a) Bacon, Lettuce and Tomato sandwich
b) Bottom Liberation Trainee
c) Bottom Lover's Tabloid

6) As a famous clunologist, you are commissioned to write a television series discussing the relevance of bottoms in assessing the personality. What will you call the programme?
a) *The Bottom on the Couch*
b) *The Bottom Line Series*
c) *The Inner Bottom*

7) What piece of clothing greatly exaggerated the female bottom during the Victorian era?
a) The corset
b) The bustle
c) The crinoline

8) What cluneal feature is famous among, and largely specific to, the Hottentot and Kalahari Bushpeople?
a) Hirsute haunches
b) Steatopygia
c) Tattooed tushes

9) A friend of the same sex as you arrives at your home just as you are about to get ready for a party. You invite him or her to come along to the party with you and offer to loan them some of your clothes, as they have just come from a building site. Then you discover that you have only one pair of clean knickers and one clean blouse/shirt. What do you do?
a) Wear the clean knickers and give them the clean shirt/blouse
b) Wear the clean blouse/shirt and give them the clean knickers
c) Give them the clean clothes and go without knickers yourself

10) The most attractive bottom you have ever seen walks past you at a party. Do you think to yourself:
a) 'Ooh, tasty'
b) 'Cor, what I wouldn't give for that'
c) 'Gosh, how extraordinary'

11) Which famous piece of literature features a one-buttocked character?
a) *The Three Musketeers*
b) *Alice in Wonderland*
c) *Candide*

12) What did Martin Luther do to ward off the devil?
a) Spit
b) Display his buttocks
c) Spill his ink and throw salt over his shoulder

13) Which British publication features the Bottom Inspectors?
a) *The Sunday Times*
b) *Viz*
c) *The Lady*

14) Which dance outraged the theatres of nineteenth century Europe with its uninhibited display of the bottom?
a) The Black Bottom
b) The CanCan
c) The Gavotte

15) Which of Chaucer's *Canterbury Tales* involves a bottom and a red hot poker?
    a) *The Weaver's Tale*
    b) *The Priest's Tale*
    c) *The Miller's Tale*

16) You are on a train, walking down the aisle, when you encounter another person coming towards you. There is no room to step aside, so you both turn and squeeze past each other. Do you turn so that:
    a) Your bottom faces their bottom
    b) Your bottom faces their front
    c) Your front faces their bottom

17) Which of these creatures has the most colourful bottom?
    a) The baboon
    b) The gibbon
    c) The orang-utan

18) Which of these cartoon characters spends the most time on his bottom?
    a) Jerry, of Tom and Jerry
    b) Porky Pig
    c) Daffy Duck

19) The Shakespearean character, Bottom, appeared in which play?
    a) *The Tempest*
    b) *As You Like It*
    c) *A Midsummer Night's Dream*

20) What was the stage name of the first dancer to dance the CanCan on a London stage?
    a) Giselle
    b) Finette
    c) Fifi

21) When you want someone to know that you really like them, do you:
    a) Snap your knicker elastic in their company
    b) Show them your bottom
    c) Smile

22) Which of the following foods most reminds you of bottoms?
   a) Tomatoes
   b) Avocadoes
   c) Cheesecake

23) Which of the following best describes your favourite method of showing your appreciation of a bottom while in public?
   a) Smacking it
   b) Pinching it
   c) Stroking it

24) The following are typical dream symbols for the bottom. Which of these symbols is most likely to appear in your dreams?
   a) The Post Office Tower
   b) An articulated lorry
   c) A Gothic mansion

25) Whose is the most photographed bottom?
   a) Rudolph Nureyev
   b) Marilyn Monroe
   c) Anneka Rice

26) Which of these famous characters did not have a bottom?
   a) Apollo
   b) The devil
   c) Pandora

27) What are the names of the muscles of the bottom?
   a) The gluteals
   b) The giblets
   c) Monosodium glutamate

28) How many muscles are in the group of bottom muscles mentioned above?
   a) Five
   b) Two
   c) Three

29) Which American actress brought the bottom into World War II?
   a) Greta Garbo
   b) Betty Grable
   c) Jane Wyman

30) What would you call a person with a fetish for biting bottoms?
   a) A Beissen Bummer
   b) An Occlusion Operator
   c) A Nether Nipper

31) If you wished to use your bottom to insult someone, would you:
   a) Display your bottom
   b) Emit a posterior eructation
   c) Kiss your fingers then touch them to your bottom

32) What would you call a one-buttocked person?
   a) Demi-derrièred
   b) Partially posteriored
   c) Pygially impoverished

33) Which of the following antics places greatest stress on the buttocks?
   a) Streaking
   b) De-bagging
   c) Mooning

34) When you want to flaunt your bottom, but must remain clothed, do you:
   a) Wear clothing that is tight round the bottom
   b) Go without knickers
   c) Both of the above

35) Which of the following invariably makes you think of bottoms?
   a) Football
   b) Nightclubs
   c) Butchers' shops

36) What is the oldest 'bum-word', still common in modern times?
   a) Ass
   b) Bum
   c) Arse

37) Which of the following was one of the large-bottomed earth goddesses worshipped by early humankind?
   a) Phoebe
   b) Hebe
   c) Gaea

38) What is the original meaning of the word 'bumf'?
   a) Paper advertisements
   b) Lavatory paper
   c) Bum fluff

39) Who composed the music, still played today, to which the CanCan was danced?
   a) J. S. Bach
   b) J. Offenbach
   c) Carl Orff

40) Which British newspaper conducted a survey of physical attraction which discovered that British women favoured the male bottom above all other features?
   a) *The Sunday Times*
   b) *The Sunday Sport*
   c) *The Sun*

41) How much time do you spend cherishing your bottom each day?
   a) Five to ten minutes
   b) No time
   c) More than ten minutes

42) Do you think your bottom:
   a) Comes from your father
   b) Comes from your mother
   c) Is a throwback

43) What was the name of the Greek goddess who was also called 'The Fair-Buttocked'?
   a) Athena
   b) Aphrodite
   c) Ariadne

44) According to the 1811 publication *The Dictionary of the Vulgar Tongue*, 'johnny bum' is a prudish substitute for what phrase?
   a) Jack ass
   b) Henry haunch
   c) Bigot bottom

45) What other part of the body is thought to be an evolutionary attempt at imitating the buttocks?
   a) The knees
   b) The hips
   c) The breasts

46) Which image of the bottom is lodged in the collective memory as a safe and comforting place to be, created initially by the mother goddess sitting upon the earth?
   a) Seat
   b) Lap
   c) Haunch

47) What was the original purpose of the phrase 'Kiss my arse'?
   a) To invite someone to make love
   b) As a friendly greeting
   c) To repel the devil

48) What item of clothing, restyled and with renewed popularity, gave both the male and female bottom increased importance and significance in the 1960s?
   a) Track suits
   b) Blue jeans
   c) Y-fronts

49) Who said that buttocks 'form a Beatitude'?
   a) Winston Churchill

   b) Thomas Nashe
   c) Paul Verlaine

50) Should a spank be given so that it hits:
   a) One buttock.
   b) Both buttocks
   c) The meeting place of lower buttocks and upper thighs

Now turn to page 125 for the answers.

CHECK YOUR SCORE
For each correct answer, give yourself or the person you are testing one point, except where otherwise indicated in the answers.

Over 50 points
You clearly have a high bottom-arousal index which either means that you are more closely related to chimpanzees than most other people, or that you've spent the majority of your life with your eyes steadfastly fixed on following the tush in front of you around. Either way, with a little more practice you could become a real weirdo. Have you noticed that people back away hurriedly when you come into a room? Get some therapy now, before it's too late.

Between 20 and 50 points
You thought this was the 'normal' category, right? Wrong. This is, in fact, the most dangerous category to be in, because it's full of people like you who've been faking their answers in the hope that no one will notice that they're secret members of Madam Martinet's Spanking Society. This quiz was designed to see straight through people like you, buster. Oh yes, you may look as if butter wouldn't melt in your mouth, but your secret's out now. We all know that behind that cool, normal-looking facade there's a weirdo desperately trying to stay in. In fact, you're probably one of those perverts who linger rather too long in the greengrocer's, squeezing each and every avocado 'just to see if it's ripe'. Well your cover's blown now, pal.

Less than 20 points
No hope, friend. You will never understand or appreciate the

finest piece of anatomy that Mother Nature has constructed in the past 100,000 years or so. Give up trying now, and become an accountant or estate agent.

7

A BUN IS FOR FUN!

Now let us set all seriousness aside and spend our remaining time together simply taking delight in the bottom. With all of its beauty, variety and innate humour, there is surely no one who could turn away from the bottom as a potential source of entertainment. So set aside all worries and dull cares and indulge, with a few like-minded friends, in an hour or two of benign and innocent frolics . . .

Cucumber and Cleavage

In this game, people with legs of equal length are paired and each pair is given a cucumber. The pair turn their backs to one another and press their bottoms (clothed or unclothed, depending upon whether you've been properly introduced) together, at the same time positioning the cucumber in the line of their cleavage(s). Each couple is lined up at a starting point and, at a signal, each pair attempts to reach the 'finish' before the other couples – with the cucumber still in place, of course.

This game may be played holding a sheet of paper in place, instead. Couples may move in a sideways shuffle or with one partner moving forward, the other moving backwards in the same direction.

Painting Parties

Further to the discussion begun in chapter three, the pleasures of pygal painting may be explored in greater depth when friends get together for a painting party. The gathering should be held at a time and in a place where no unforeseen interference will cause embarrassment. Plenty of food and beverages should be supplied as well as a selection of non-toxic make-up and body paints. The participants should attend either already painted – in which case they should be prepared to display their artwork – or they may find a painting partner at the party. It is necessary to work in pairs, though larger groups are sometimes successful.

To liven up the proceedings, a theme may be announced and a competition for the best thematic bottom held, with prizes awarded. For instance, Rainbow Rumps, British Landscapes or Old Master Reproductions are themes that have been especially successful in recent years. Most painted people like to keep a record of what their bottom looked like and, for this purpose, several sheets of A3 size white paper should be kept on hand. At the end of the party, the painted person simply sits on the paper and rocks gently from side to side in order to leave a clear imprint of their painting on the paper. As an alternative, instant photography may be used, of course (note: do not take the film to your local chemist, unless he/she is also invited to the gala) but it lacks the vigorous enthusiasm of imprinting.

Shave 'n' Paint Parties

Similar to Painting Parties, but in this case at least one bottom has to be hairy (so that it may be shaved). The same guidelines apply with the added precaution that only electric razors are used. The themes may be somewhat bolder in this type of party, including Famous Politicians, Frightening Faces or Cartoon Characters. Imprinting is very successful with shaved 'n' painted bottoms, the hairs often adding an unusual texture to the final outcome.

Photocopy Chains

First, make ten A3 size photocopies of your bottom and send them, anonymously, to ten of your friends and acquaintances.

Include a letter advising them to photocopy their own bottom ten times and send *it* off to ten more people. All such letters should be typed, unsigned and contain the following paragraph:

'Sharing a facsimile of your bottom will do no harm to you and will greatly enhance the lives of every person who receives it. They will feel inspired to perpetuate the sharing process and, before long, the whole world will feel jovial and gentle. Your contribution will help!'

Please note that all photocopiers should be wiped clean both before and after the copy session.

Photocopy Chains

Jacksies in a Jam

Something for the younger and more athletic among the population. The goal of this game is simply to squeeze as many bottoms, clothed or unclothed, into as tight a space as possible. Some possible jams are: a bath tub, a phone booth, a mini car, through a window or in a paddling pool. The game becomes more gratifying if the local media is called in to cover the story, and if several local councillors, school governors or politicians can be induced to participate.

Shuffle Bun

For some reason, this game creates instant hysteria – yet it is simply and eminently wholesome. The players remove their shoes and sit on the floor with their legs stretched out in front of them. A 'caller' announces the exact purpose of the game, which can take many forms, before signalling the start. Now the players 'walk' or shuffle on their bottoms according to the instructions given. For instance, the game may be a simple race from one side of the room to the other. Or it may be a rhythmic race to the accompaniment of rock and roll music, with the caller disqualifying those who fail to keep rhythm. Better still, though more complicated, is the combination of racing with music in which the caller announces a forward, backward or sideways movement in any order, to create a sort of bottom-based square dance. The final minute of the music is, in this case, devoted to completing the course with all players attempting to reach the 'finish' first.

Streaking

Streaking involves the removal of all or most of one's clothing and a subsequent display of one's nudity in a public place. The act is usually performed while on the run, or through some other means of locomotion. While not focusing specifically on the bottom, streaking does usually reveal the bottom and certainly the bottom of a streaker receives considerable attention from the 'audience', those being streaked at.

Although usually confined to the younger members of the population, streaking is a thrilling pastime which has hardly begun to fulfill its playful potential. There certainly seems to be no good reason to discriminate against potential streakers merely on the spurious grounds of age, and if this harmless and health-giving sport were to be encouraged in homes for the elderly, it would no doubt serve as a tonic and offer invigoration for our sadly greying nation. While uncertain of the precise legality of streaking, and not wishing to encourage delinquent behaviour by any means, it is recommended that any potential streaker first checks his or her precise legal position with the local chief constable, who no doubt has established licensing procedures for this sort of event.

Group Streaking: the comradeship of others helps novices in particular to maintain their courage while performing the act. It also enables the 'capture' of a site – such as a fountain, corridor or park bench – which can sometimes add emphasis and subtle visual counterpoint to the entertainment.

Motorised Streaking: motorcycles, mopeds, convertible cars and even bicycles have all been used to add to the expressive nature of a streak. Lone, coupled or group streaks are possible on these vehicles. No report has yet been received of a train or tube carriage being overrun with streakers. Similarly, an omnibus, particularly an open-top sort, would seem an obvious choice for an enthusiastic streaker.

Occasion Streaking: special occasions as diverse as graduation ceremonies, orchestral concerts and society funerals have triggered the streaking urge at one time or another. Psychologists have not fully explored this urge though they conjecture that it is comprised of some element of exhibitionism, jealousy of those already receiving attention and a goofy sense of humour.

Hidden Charms

In this party game, the guests are formed into two teams of four people each, with the remaining guests participating as what we shall call 'charmers'. These charmers take it in turn to step forward to face the two teams. Once there, the team members may ask the charmer a total of three questions about the knickers they are wearing *or* they may pass one hand firmly and rapidly over the charmer's bottom *once* only. From the information they receive, the panels must try to guess what sort of knickers the charmer is wearing, if any. Each team is given a set of eight cards; on each card is written one of the following descriptions:

Cotton Cover-ups
Silk Scintillators
Canvas Crushers
Bun Huggers
Rubber Rudities
Leather Lewdies
Naughty Nudies
Added Extras

The teams are allowed two minutes to question the charmer and one minute to discuss their decision. At the end of this time, each team must raise one of the eight cards as their guess at the type of knickers the charmer is wearing. The charmer has final say as to whether a guess is correct or not, though they should expect, on some occasions, to be pressurised into displaying the correct answer. When all the charmers have had a go, the team with the greatest number of correct guesses is the winner. Awards are discretionary.

Pucker Power

In this game the serious matter of tone testing is turned to humorous display. The players all pledge to clench an object of their choice firmly between their cluneal cheeks, using the inward exertion of gluteal tension. The players must then undertake to carry this object to a designated place in the room and deposit it there, without once dropping the object. Onlookers may wish to bet small amounts on their favoured winner.

Mooning

Not strictly speaking a game, mooning has a very game-like effect on most participants and observers. Mooning involves a total, though brief, display of the naked buttocks and gains its name from the resemblance of the bared buttocks to a large, glowing moon. It has advantages over streaking in that it may be accomplished and concealed within a very short space of time. Mooning is also a highly versatile activity: it may be used to delight, to amuse or even to issue a social snub or put-down when in sophisticated company. And because it is physically and temporally concise, it may be directed at one or more persons with well-aimed precision.

Mooning may be combined with many other bottomnal entertainments. Painted moons may be displayed to add cultural value to the event and mobile mooning may be performed to entertain a crowded carpark or a bus full of pensioners on a tour. Indeed, there is no end to the creativity one may lavish upon the worship of Diana, the moon-goddess.

Cheek By Jowl

This game requires at least eight people before it is worth playing; all players remain fully clothed throughout. One person is given whispered instructions by a referee to 'go out to the garden shed and get a rake' or 'go up to the small bedroom and find the slippers' or even 'take the dog for a walk in the garden'. Before these instructions are carried out, however, the other players must form a queue behind this first player. The second player must place his or her side of face (jowl) or the top of their head against the first player's bottom (cheek). Each player in turn must attach themselves in the same way to the player in front of them.

Once this construction of players has been achieved, the first player may set out to perform the whispered task. The referee accompanies the tangle of people to ensure that the cheek-by-jowl contact is maintained at all times. (A more precise code of play may be devised for each game, according to the spirit of the players.) The first player may move fast or slow and may try to confound the other players or not. However, the most simple of movements is made difficult and humorous by the tail of people linked to the first layer.

Rear View Rumpus

A number of costume tails are arranged on a table where all the players may see them. These may vary considerably in style and shape, but they must each be of a small to medium size, for reasons which will become apparent. All but one of the players then close their eyes and turn their backsides to the table. The remaining player becomes the compère and proceeds to attach a tail to each player. When all the tails are attached the players may open their eyes and mingle freely with one another. At no time are the players allowed to touch their own rear or their new tail and neither are they allowed to look back at themselves in a mirror. Instead, they must try to remember all the tails which they saw on the table and compare them with all of the tails which they can now see on their companions.

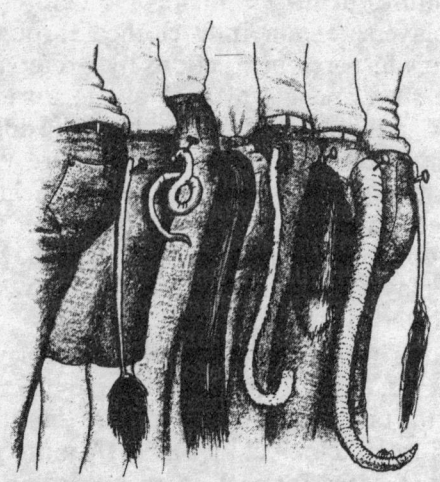

Line-up for Rear View Rumpus

When a given length of time has passed (fifteen minutes is a suitable period), the compère asks each person if they can guess which tail they are wearing. The person or persons who have accurately deduced the missing tail receive a pre-arranged award.

Lovable Limericks

You don't have to be a poet to write a limerick. All that is needed is a good sense of humour, a twisted view of life (which you've already demonstrated by reading this far) and, perhaps, a rhyming dictionary. Of course, the limericks you create should include the subject of our studies, the bottom, and may be written with a friend or friends. Here are a couple to get you started:

> There was a young woman named Fanny
> Whose skill with her hands was uncanny.
> She knew how to spank,
> She knew how to bank,
> And that was before she met Danny!

> A doctor who studied interiors
> Was terribly fond of posteriors.
> But while pinching the botty
> Of lovely Nurse Dotty
> He caught some unfriendly bacterias.

> There was an old woman named Lap
> Who gave her rear end a big slap
> 'There's not enough meat
> On this old woman's seat,
> And the wrinkles could line a big map.'

> There was a young woman named June
> Whose bottom resembled the moon
> So she made lots of pictures
> Which broke lots of strictures
> But won her an Order of Clune.

How Heavy the Haunches?

This game is exceptionally funny to play but not altogether resolved in its outcome. The point is to guess the weight of a person's rump and then award points or whatever to the person who came nearest to the correct figure. But – and it's a big butt – how does one weigh a rump?

There is the Archimedes Principle which involves a very full bucket of water set in an even larger bucket or bowl. The favoured rump is slowly lowered into the freezing fluid to the point at which all agree the bottom is immersed (and this, in fact, may be the high spot of the game). The water overflows from the bucket into the larger bucket and the rump is then removed. The amount of water displaced by the derrière should tell us something . . . But it doesn't. Not, that is, unless you already know the weight per cubic inch of an Official and Standard buttock.

So, while remaining an authentic scientific query, bottom-weighing also continues to be a hilarious and riotous game, with few rules and – so far – no answers. If you or any of your cluneal colleagues come up with an accurate way of ascertaining the weight of a bottom, please submit your suggestions for possible publication in the next edition of *The Book of Bottoms*.

ANSWERS TO THE CLUNOLOGY QUIZ

1. b) *Barbarella*.
2. a) No, no, no. You've got it all wrong. Remember – these people are *Italians* – they do this sort of thing all the time, and double up on Sundays. So loosen up and enjoy your holiday, or you'll be on sedatives inside a week. *Minus three points*.
   b) Right, that's more like it! But don't be too passive – try slapping the nearest person on the face (it doesn't have to be the person who pinched you) just to keep the thing moving along. Italians know that slaps aren't really serious (note: if the nearest person is German, disregard this advice). *One point*.
   c) Yes, yes, yes! You've got it! All the makings of a first-class bum fetishist! *Three points*.
3. We cheated – they all are.
4. a) You've got to be joking! What kind of weirdos, deviants and perverts do you think you're going to attract with a name like that? Get sensible: *Minus three points*.
   b) Not much better. How about putting a little class into your ass – try . . . *One point*.
   c) 'Gluteal Assessment Practitioner' is the very essence of what it's all about – quality, breeding, style astronomical bills . . . it says it all. *Five points*.
5. a) Who are you trying to kid, goody two-shoes? Don't give us that innocent little number – it's quite obvious that you're a deeply disturbed clunopath with voyeuristic tendencies who's desperately trying to cover it up. Well,

it just doesn't work. We know what you're *really* like. *Minus three points.*

b) Nice one. Progressive, forward-looking, politically aware. Very right-on. But stupid. *One point.*

c) The obvious answer. Except that people who buy that kind of tabloid normally haven't quite progressed yet to joined-up writing. So who's reading *this* aloud to you? *Minus one point.*

6. a) Sigmund would be proud of you. Unfortunately, no one else is. *One point.*

b) Are you an accountant? Well you think like one. *One point.*

c) You will obviously do well inside the management of satellite television. *One point.*

7. b) The bustle.

8. b) Steatopygia.

9. a) Logical, but not very exciting, is it? In fact, you're downright dull and unadventurous. Why are you bothering going to the party, in any case? You'd probably get more excitement out of curling up with a hot cup of milk and watching *I Love Lucy* reruns on television. *Minus three points.*

b) You're rather bizarre, not to say downright kinky, aren't you? I mean, ask yourself, why is it so important that your friend should wear clean knickers, while you're not going to do so yourself? Surely better not to wear any, and . . . oh, never mind. *Three points.*

c) Very adventurous. But are you sure it's that kind of party? *Five points.*

10. a) A bit vulgar, aren't you? A few lessons in elementary manners would not go amiss. *Two points.*

b) No, no, no. You've obviously bought this book for all the wrong reasons. And we did try *so hard* to keep that sort of reader away from it. Go back to reading your fish and chip wrappers. *Minus three points.*

c) Yes! The correct response of the professional

clunologist – detached, scientific, and impartial. *Well done! Three points.*

11. c) *Candide.*
12. b) Display his buttocks.
13. b) *Viz.*
14. b) The CanCan.
15. c) *The Miller's Tale.*
16. There is no correct answer, but your manner of passage indicates much about your personality:
    a) You have a deeply-repressed libido which needs immediate attention. *Three points if you agree to go into therapy right now, otherwise minus three points.*
    b) You are an exhibitionist. *Three points.*
    c) The best means of passage for a professional bottom person. *Five points.*
17. b) The gibbon.
18. a) Jerry, of Tom and Jerry.
19. c) *A Midsummer Night's Dream.*
20. b) Finette.
21. a) A pernicious little habit, well worth curing yourself of. *Minus three points.*
    b) Please leave your name and address with the publisher and we will be in touch for a full inspection. *Five points.*
    c) Frankly, having read this far in the book, we just don't believe you. What are you trying to hide? *Minus five points.*
22. a) Illogical; unless, that is, you're a very heavy spanker. *Minus one point.*
    b) Slightly more logical, but *green bottoms*? *One point.*
    c) OK, *everything* reminds you of bottoms, right? *Three points.*
23. a) When you get out of jail, start right from the beginning

again, from potty-training classes onwards. *Minus three points*.
b) If you have Italian blood in you, fine. Otherwise, ease up on the pizza, or it's the funny farm for you, my friend. *Minus one point*.
c) Only acceptable as long as you are already on first-name terms. Not generally considered to be a good way to make new friends. *Minus one point*.

a) No, wrong dream, or more likely, wrong book. Try exchanging this one for anything by Jeffrey Archer. *Minus three points*.
b) Fine, fine, just lie down over there please, the nurse will be in presently with your injection and nice comfy jumpsuit. *One point*.
c) This is a little confusing – if you're really thinking about bottoms when you dream about gothic mansions, does it mean that you're thinking about gothic mansions when you dream about bottoms? Please get some help. *Minus three points*.

25. b) Marilyn Monroe.

26. b) The devil.

27. a) The gluteals.

28. c) Three.

29. b) Betty Grable.

30. a) This indicates a strong desire to get down there on the floor and join in. Stop it right now. *Minus three points*.
b) Good, good, very acceptable clunological terminology, go to the top of the class. *Five points*.
c) A trifle whimsical, don't you think? Get real! *Minus one point*.

31. a) Mooning is not a terribly practical way of giving insult, unless you are well out of reach of the other person. And it just might be misunderstood as an invitation to go riding. *Minus one point*.

b) Yes, but can you do this *at will*? *Really*? *Minus one point*.
c) Refined, but effective. You are clearly a gifted giver of insults. *Three points*.

24. All alternatives are acceptable, although (c) 'Pygially impoverished' implies class distinction and is therefore more in vogue at the present time, and earns you *three points*.

33. c) Mooning.

34. c) is obviously the best option, but indicates a nasty, animal-like and ruthless streak in you that quite frankly, we didn't know you had. *Three points*.

35. a) Sexually, you are bewildered and mixed-up. Football is not about bottoms, it is about violence and money. Remember that, and try again after the therapy. *Minus three points*.
b) A healthy response. Thank goodness *someone*'s normal around here. *Five points for being normal*.
c) You can*not* be serious. Hopefully, you're *not* serious. Either that, or the Home for the Criminally Insane is missing one inmate. Eat a lot of Rump steaks, do you? Name's not Norman Bates by any chance? *Minus five points*.

36. c) Arse.

37. c) Gaea.

38. b) Lavatory paper.

39. b) J. Offenbach.

40. a) *The Sunday Times*.

41. a) Barely adequate, is it? But there's hope yet, so re-read chapter three. *One point*.
b) Shame on you! May your bum sag, your flesh wither and flap, and your buttocks become ingrowing. You deserve it. *Minus three points*.

c) Attaboy! You'll be entering our Hall of Fame in a few years' time – care to give us a sneak preview now? *Three points.*

42. a) Fine if you're male, not so good if you're female, or if your poor old dad lost a buttock in the war. *One point.*
    b) Fine either way, but be careful she doesn't ask for it back. *One point.*
    c) This sounds really distasteful and repellant. Please do not send us photos of it, or reveal yourself in public any more than is absolutely necessary. Strongly urge you to consider having your bottom-half entombed in one of those concrete-lined radioactive dumps they're building all over the place. If the locals don't object, that is. *Minus three points.*

43. b) Aphrodite.

44. a) Jack ass.

45. c) The breasts.

46. b) Lap.

47. c) To repel the devil.

48. b) Blue jeans.

49. c) Paul Verlaine.

50. b) Both buttocks.

PHOTOGRAPH CREDITS

Rex Features Ltd

The Telegraph Colour Library

MORE HUMOUR TITLES AVAILABLE FROM HODDER AND STOUGHTON PAPERBACKS

☐	49473 X	Roger Planer & Richard McBrien How to Give Up Sex	£2.50
☐	49474 8	Steve Wright It's Another True Story	£2.50
☐	50813 7	Ronnie Barker It's Hello From Him	£2.99
☐	50809 9	David Renwick But I Digress	£2.50

All these books are available at your local bookshop or newsagent, or can be ordered direct from the publisher. Just tick the titles you want and fill in the form below.

Prices and availability subject to change without notice.

HODDER AND STOUGHTON PAPERBACKS, P.O. Box 11, Falmouth, Cornwall.

Please send cheque or postal order, and allow the following for postage and packing:

U.K. – 55p for one book, plus 22p for the second book, and 14p for each additional book ordered up to a £1.75 maximum.

B.F.P.O. and EIRE – 55p for the first book, plus 22p for the second book, and 14p per copy for the next 7 books, 8p per book thereafter.

OTHER OVERSEAS CUSTOMERS – £1.00 for the first book, plus 25p per copy for each additional book.

NAME ....

ADDRESS ....

....